Peace for THE JOURNEY

Peace for THE JOURNEY
in the pleasure of his company

F. ELAINE OLSEN

NyreePress

© 2010, 2014 by Elaine Olsen. All rights reserved.

Cover Design by Tekeme Studios.

Published by NyreePress Literary Group (www.nyreepress.com). NyreePress functions only as book publisher. As such, the ultimate design, content, editorial accuracy, and views expressed or implied in this work are those of the author.

No part of this publication may be reproduced, stored in a retrieval system, or transmitted in any way by any means—electronic, mechanical, photocopy, recording, or otherwise—without the prior permission of the copyright holder, except as provided by USA copyright law.

Unless otherwise noted, all scriptures are taken from the *Holy Bible, New International Version*, *NIV*. Copyright © 1973, 1978, 1984 by Biblica, Inc.™ Used by permission of Zondervan. All rights reserved worldwide. WWW.ZONDERVAN.COM

Print ISBN: 978-0-9906662-0-2
Library of Congress Catalog Card Number: 2014947606

To my peace, Jesus Christ

I hold my pen for you alone.

Contents

acknowledgments xi

introduction: a promised peace xiii

1. peace in the pardon 1
the amazing confrontation of grace 2
the glorious wonderful of a heart's break 6
"who touched me?" a bleeding issue 10
a spring's visit to a winter's prison 14
my ashes, God's Spirit 18

2. peace in the mirror 21
the hope of forced perception 22
God's plow, my longing 25
sacred mystery, intended ministry 29
pressing in 33
crossroads 37

3. peace in the desert 41
a call to the desert 42
a crossroads in the desert 46

a turn toward the better (part one) 50
a turn toward the better (part two) 54
the backside of forty 57

4. peace in the waters 61

from bitter to better 62
the beauty of a backward glance 66
a sacred reduction 70
the glorious renaissance of a flooded fury 74
a sea's deliverance 78

5. peace in the suffering 83

unseen glances 84
a cup that would not pass 88
a sacred covering 92
the painful truth 96
through and through 100

6. peace in the mountains 105

a peaked perspective 106
keepers of the light 110
a worthy climb 113
packing up a vacation, punctuating a week 117
proximity to presence 120

7. peace at church 125

posturing our hearts for a sabbath rest 126
sacramental second helpings 130
a sacred doing 134
come. tarry. go. 138
kingdom carriers 141

8. peace around the table with the ancients 145
    lunching with the ancients 146
    finding our voices 150
    a treasured storing 154
    praying like ms. iris 158
    concluding exhortations 161

9. peace at home 165
    a well-seeded heart 166
    a golden moment 170
    brotherly love 174
    benedictions 178
    where the heart is 182

10. peace on the road 187
    on the road with Jesus 188
    love tied to a tree 191
    a winter's run 195
    a gracious plenty 199
    a morning's glory 202

conclusion: a leaving peace 207

endnotes 209

Acknowledgments

My gracious thanks to the many companions who walk the journey with me and who continually point me to the Author of peace. You have given me the courage to write my life in living color and to live it all the more:

Mom and Dad, you gave me my first roadmap to peace.

Billy, you opened up my heart to love again and led me home to peace.

Nick, Colton, Jadon, and Amelia, you are worthy of this mother's continual pursuit of peace.

Bill and Rosalie, you exemplify the simple and quiet trust of a life lived in peace.

My Tuesday "ancients," you boast the years and shaping of having walked with peace.

My Bible study girls, you come alongside me in search of peace through the exploration of God's Word.

My blog readers, you faithfully return to find peace at my cyber address.

*My three "Js"—Juanita, Judith, and Joyful—*you hold out peace to me when the chaos begins its crowding.

Jeffery Minnish, you beautifully captured a portrait of peace for the front cover of this book at Grantham Farms.

Susan Hood, your vision of peace is through the lens of your camera, and you graciously share that vision within the pages of this book.

Linda Gilden, your editing of my words and your encouragement to my spirit have brought peace to the process of publication.

Dr. Maxie Dunnam, you continue to champion my pen because of your fierce championing for the cause of peace throughout the world.

Beth Moore, your passionate pursuit to know the Author of peace has challenged and strengthened me in my quest for the same.

Alicia Chole, you've guided me toward making peace with my anonymous seasons.

My eighth grade history teacher, Mrs. Edwards, in 1980 you walked your peace into a classroom and scripted a word of hope and possibility into my yearbook and across my heart: "Dear Elaine, I have discovered a new and exciting talent that you have this year. I expect you to be a successful writer one day. You really have the ability."

And finally, *you—the reader—*your search for peace has led you here. I am grateful for your trust and consider it my highest privilege to point you to peace—to Jesus Christ, our Lord and Savior, in whom all things live and move and have their being. You make me want to be a better seeker, thinker, writer, and sojourner for the journey.

Introduction: a promised peace

He will stand and shepherd his flock in the strength of the Lord, in the majesty of the name of the Lord his God. And they will live securely, for then his greatness will reach to the ends of the earth. And he will be their peace.

—Micah 5:4–5

For over a decade now, I've been closing my correspondence with the benediction, "peace for the journey." I'm not sure as to the reason behind its beginning, but I think it had something to do with the fact that my journey, in that season of living, hosted a fragmented peace. It still does. There are little pieces of peace here and there, but rarely is it constant.

I want peace. I imagine you feel the same way. Perhaps that is the motivation behind your picking up this book.

Peace is a sought-after commodity in a world overflowing with chaotic dissonance; still and yet, it eludes us. We all want it, yet so few of us possess any lasting measure of it. Why? It is because we are a people who have inaccurately assessed the means for acquiring it. We level our quest for peace within the boundaries of the temporal, without acknowledging that true and lasting peace can only be found in the "pressing in" towards the eternal.

Peace isn't a concept. Peace is a person. Accordingly, we cannot purchase peace's portion, even though our market-driven society begs to differ. We can spend a lifetime and a fortune on coddling preferences that paint a momentary calm, but for peace to truly govern a life's journey, peace requires an investment beyond the bank account.

Lasting peace requires a relationship.

To walk a pilgrimage *in* peace, we must walk *with* peace. Scripture identifies peace not just by its characteristics but, more profoundly, by giving peace a name—Jesus Christ

(Ephesians 2:14). Holding him in our hearts moves peace within reach. The more we know Jesus, the more we know peace.

I've known Jesus for a long season. I cannot remember a time when I questioned his authenticity. He's always been real to me. Accordingly, he's always been an easy find. Unpacking his presence in my everyday life isn't a stretch. Indeed, there have been seasons of my intentional neglect regarding his presence, but my refusal to look his way doesn't mean that he isn't looking in mine.

Jesus Christ intends to be known. He has created our hearts for the same. When we finally arrive at the conclusion that lasting peace walks in partnership with the Creator of our souls, then peace begins to sew its covering over the chaos that so easily entangles our flesh.

Peace doesn't fully measure out with that conclusion. It begins there—seeding its truth for further blooms that display their beauty along the way and as we go. Peace is a daily walk; it is a journey of trust that is content to wrap a twenty-four hour period with the unwrapping of the only God who can be known. And when that happens—when the unpacking of heaven's sacred treasure becomes the norm rather than the exception—then "peace for the journey" is no longer a curiosity. "Peace for the journey" becomes our reality.

This is my hope for the book that you now cradle in your hands. I want peace to be your portion for the journey ahead. I want you to know your Jesus in deeper measure. I hope you find him here.

In the mountains. In the desert. In the waters. At church and around the table with friends. On the road and at home. In the pain and in the pardon. In the mirror and then some more. I have found him in all of those places. My journey has afforded me the beauty of all manner of detours throughout my forty-three years of walking its course. All of them have brought me to this one moment in time—a moment of sharing with you some personal snapshots of a well-worn faith and the faithful companion who has allowed me the privilege of unpacking his presence in my everyday.

It is my joy and highest honor to point you to Jesus. Nothing in my life exceeds the worth of knowing him and of sharing that knowing with you via my pen. What you hold in your hands is my offering toward that end.

When you hold Jesus, friends, you hold everything. My prayer for you is to walk always in the truth and joy of that holding. May the blossoms and blooms of God's everlasting peace companion and cover you in lavish portion as you go. Thank you for sharing the road with me.

Introduction: a promised peace

As always,
Peace for the journey~

Elaine

P.S. A note about this book . . .

The reflections contained within these pages are designed to stand alone and don't need to be read in sequential order. If your life has taken a detour to the desert, choose a reflection located in the section "peace in the desert." If a mirror is calling for your introspection, take a peek in the section "peace in the mirror." This book is meant to be a resource for you as you go about your ordinary life with your extraordinary Jesus.

If you desire to take your pondering a step beyond the daily reading, "a further pause" is offered after each concluding prayer to deepen and strengthen your personal application of the principles laid out in each reflection. You may want to consider using a journal or notebook to chronicle your thoughts, as space for answers is limited.

Finally, the book lends itself to times of personal study but also can serve as a practical resource for small groups desiring to walk corporately in and with the peace of Jesus Christ.

Either way, the pleasure of his company awaits you.

Peace in the pardon

Jesus straightened up and asked her, "Woman, where are they? Has no one condemned you?" "No one, sir," she said. "Then neither do I condemn you," Jesus declared. "Go now and leave your life of sin."

—John 8:10–11

 *the amazing confrontation of grace*

On hearing it, many of his disciples said, "This is a hard teaching. Who can accept it?" Aware that his disciples were grumbling about this, Jesus said to them, "Does this offend you? What if you see the Son of man ascend to where he was before! The Spirit gives life; the flesh counts for nothing. The words I have spoken to you are spirit and they are life. Yet there are some of you who do not believe."
—John 6:60–64a

I made a two-year-old cry this morning.

I didn't mean to make her cry. Singing about the amazing grace of God isn't supposed to bring one to tears, at least not her kind of tears, but this morning it did.

Perhaps I sang it too loudly. Perhaps too shrilly. Perhaps too full of a truth that exceeded the silence of the moment. Regardless of the reasons behind her tears, they came in full measure toward the end of my serenade, accompanied by her tender proclamation to her grandmother, "I don't like that song."

It made my heart smile, and then it made me think.

The amazing grace of Jesus Christ is a confrontational message. It is meant to stir a response in the hearts of those who sit within earshot of the proclamation. Jesus Christ didn't go all the way to Calvary and back to keep us paralyzed by its truth. Grace is meant to evoke a response in each one of us.

For some, grace swallows sweetly. For some, it's a longer chew. For others, grace doesn't swallow—amazing or otherwise. It is simply too big a bite for a stomach that is content to gnaw on the stony rations of an uncomplicated understanding. Just ask them—those "followers" of Christ who were eyewitnesses to the real-time unfolding of grace's "amazing." Some would immediately begin its unwrapping. Some would live with it for a season before coming around to acceptance. Some would simply balk at the weight of it and run in the opposite direction. The "them" of Jesus' day are no different from the "us" of this day.

We like to think that our responses to Jesus would have been different had we been there. That somehow we would have immediately taken to the truth of his living witness. But I don't think the benefit of a two-thousand-year hindsight has birthed a better faith in most of us. Why? It is because we have the truth of Christ's living witness in our midst. He is here among us; he didn't vanish on a hillside to never be seen again. He has been presenting himself and his amazing grace to humanity throughout the existence of time. You and I sit on the backside of grace's redeeming finish; still and yet, its truth isn't an easy cloaking for many. It is a hard teaching in our time, even as it was during its genesis on Judean soil so long ago.

Does this mean that grace no longer works? That the amazing of John Newton's 1779 penned reflection lacks in its truthful punctuation about the completed work of the cross? That our many words about the Word have somehow lost their potency—their capacity and strength to transform?

Not at all.

Grace is still amazing. Two thousand years of testing its waters hasn't diminished its effectiveness. Grace's truth remains, despite man's refusal to acknowledge its worth. Grace is as grace has always been.

Confrontational.

Thus, some will receive it and some won't, because confrontation pushes the issue of our consent for God's holy consecration of our lives. Grace stands at the door of a heart and knocks and pleads and invites and offers, but never will it hammer its insistence into the heart of unwillingness. The cross of Jesus Christ will never force its grace into the will of an unbeliever. It only forces a choice in the matter.

Acceptance or rejection. There is no middle ground when it comes to the amazing grace of an amazing God. Hearing his truth requires a response.

When I was a teenager, I walked my definite response to an altar one wintry night in Alabama during a youth retreat. It wouldn't be the last time I walked that pilgrimage. I'm still walking it. I did so today. Not because I have finally come to the conclusion of what an "amazing grace" means, but rather because grace and all its amazing is worthy of my bended knee and my heart's pause that cries out a prayer or two of unashamed thankfulness.

Even when it's loud. Even when its understanding is a hard swallow. Even when it elicits unexpected tears. And especially when the fullness of its truth exceeds the worth of a world's silence.

Amazing grace! How sweet the sound!
That saved a wretch like me!
I once was lost, but now am found;
Was blind, but now I see.[1]

Peace for the Journey

How glad I am for the amazing confrontation of God's grace with my heart. May I never lose the wonder behind its unwrapping. May I always speak the witness of its truth. I pray the same for you. Thus, I offer my plea this day to the One who created us with grace in mind—

Intersect our hearts, Father, with grace's amazing witness this week. Fill our mouths with the sweetness of its taste. Loudly knock its truth upon the door of our wills so as to drown out the world's insistence. When it's hard to understand, when it's difficult to accept, present your grace to us in a way that swallows easily and that portions fully. May our tears pour the witness of understanding rather than the wetness of confusion. Gently wrap our faith in the mystery of Love's redeeming work and then give us the ample courage to tie the bow. What we now know in part, we will one day fully grasp. Keep us in reverent anticipation of that final revelation. Amen.

A further pause . . .

- Describe your initial confrontation with the "amazing" behind God's grace. What surprised you the most? What was your response?

- Why is grace a "confrontational" message?

- What are some of the possible reasons behind people's varying responses to God's offer of grace?

- Jesus spent his earthly pilgrimage confronting people with his amazing grace. Take time to explore the following passages and record how his grace was a "hard teaching" to absorb.

    Luke 4:14–30

    John 3:1–21

    John 6:25–70

    John 7:14–53

 *the glorious wonderful of a heart's break*

When a woman who had lived a sinful life in that town learned that Jesus was eating at the Pharisee's house, she brought an alabaster jar of perfume, and as she stood behind him at his feet weeping, she began to wet his feet with her tears. Then she wiped them with her hair, kissed them and poured perfume on them.

—Luke 7:37–38

"Mommy, that movie breaks my heart."
"Why?"
"Because it was so wonderful."
"Why was it so wonderful?"
"Because in the end, the king lets her make music."
"Say that again, Amelia, so Mommy can remember it for always."
"Because in the end, the king lets her make music."

This was the conversation I had with my daughter last night after she had finished watching *The Little Mermaid: Ariel's Beginning*. I meant to watch it with her, but a lengthy phone conversation took me away from the moment. She came to me with an unusual blend of emotions—tears in her eyes and a smile on her face. There was something familiar about her look. It is one I've worn over the years. Sadness and joy all mixed up within the welling of a wetness that now poured down her cheeks.

Her emotions may seem an odd coupling to those who have never known the glorious wonderful of a heart's break. But I have tasted such a portion, for I have known a great loss, only to be surprised in the end by a great wonderful.

A great grace.

Atlantica—the magical waters of mermaids and talking sea creatures—had lost its capacity to sing. Not because it didn't hold a melody within its waters, but rather because a tragic death had beaten its drum upon her shores. Loudly and profoundly it marched, sending song's breath to a watery grave, to be buried deep within the unseen sands of an untouched grief.

Peace in the pardon

Pain does that. It buries. It may burst forth in all manner of wild expressions at the time of sorrow, but it almost always finds a way to, at least temporarily, suspend the song. When death of any kind marches its cadence upon the soil of our souls, it buries. It digs deeply and cries hard and grasps for fragments of control that don't allow the music its voice.

But here is the truth of the eternal song. Once the music has made its way into a heart, no amount of throwing and crying and denying its pulse can keep it buried forever. We can go to the grave refusing it a voice, but in the end, the music remains. It will find its chorus, even without our participation, because the King's music is meant to be sung.

Not long ago, there was a woman who yearned for her song's return. For an extensive season it had remained buried beneath the sands of her untouched grief. Almost forgotten. Almost submerged beyond retrieval. Almost too hard and too painful a reckoning. Almost.

But there was something about this Jesus that struck a chord deep within her. Remote and distant at first, but stirring nonetheless. A stirring worthy of an offering. A stirring worthy of her tear-stained kisses and her hair's gentle caress. A stirring worthy of her walk of shame before men and, at last, before her Savior. A stirring worthy of the search, because in the end, the King allowed her the glorious wonderful of a heart's break.

In the end, he gave her his music.

Then Jesus said to her, "Your sins are forgiven. . . . Your faith has saved you; go in peace."
—Luke 8:48–50

I know the woman. I've seen her before. Not just on the pages of Scripture, but in the mirror staring back at me.

God has allowed me the glorious wonderful of a heart's break. The surrender was painful, and indeed, my heart was shattered into a thousand pieces and scattered throughout the sands of a sinful disobedience. The broken pieces seemed irretrievable, too deeply buried and too hidden for discovery. And when God's music had all but diminished to a faint whisper within me, I almost gave way to despair—to neglecting the single chord that held as my anchor despite my disregard for his presence.

But then I heard that Jesus was in town, and I was compelled to get to his feet. The closer I moved towards him, the louder the melody within me grew. And once I saw him, the chasm that existed between my great need and his great wonder was palpable and strong, truthful and tender. I knelt in tearful surrender and was surprised by the gracious and great grace from this King who has been letting me make his music ever since.

Peace for the Journey

A sinner. Her King. A surrender. His music.
The glorious wonderful of a heart's break.
May it be so for each one of us this day; thus, I pray—

Make your music, Father; sing through me. Those notes that you seeded in my heart so long ago, play them as you will and weave them into your eternal chorus with a blending that sings sweetly in the ear and with a grace that harbors gently within the soul. Thank you for the gift of a difficult journey and for the season that turned me inside out, allowing me a hard reckoning with the truth of Calvary's gift. You have turned my mourning into dancing, and for the rest of my earthly days, I commit my voice to the song of your renown. Amen.

Peace in the pardon

A further pause . . .

- ❧ Take time to read the full account of the woman's journey to Jesus' feet as found in Luke 7:36–50.

- ❧ The moment extended beyond the exchange between the woman and Jesus to include the other guests at the table. What was the parallel lesson that Jesus used to teach them about forgiveness?

- ❧ How is our love for Jesus tied into his forgiveness of our sins?

- ❧ Write out the two concluding phrases that Jesus spoke to the woman in verses 48 and 50.

- ❧ Describe the moment when Jesus first sang these words into your heart—the glorious wonderful of *your* heart's break. Does the song still sing as vividly and as real as it once did?

- ❧ Bring your remembrance to God this day and ask him to sing his message of love over your heart. "Your sins are forgiven, your faith has saved you. Go in peace."

 *"who touched me?" a bleeding issue*

As Jesus was on his way, the crowds almost crushed him. And a woman was there who had been subject to bleeding for twelve years, but no one could heal her. She came up behind him and touched the edge of his cloak, and immediately her bleeding stopped. "Who touched me?" Jesus asked. When they all denied it, Peter said, "Master, the people are crowding and pressing against you." But Jesus said, "Someone touched me; I know that power has gone out of me."

—Luke 8:42–46

She had an "issue."

I have mine. You have yours.

Hers was blood.

Ours are other things—blacks and blues and hues of all manner of issues. Regardless of their color, they still bleed red. And if not tended to by the Healer, they will continue their hemorrhage toward eventual destruction.

I know. I suffer with an "issue" right now. And in the midst of my flowing pain, I walked a story tonight that spoke a tender portion of healing truth over my wounds.

The stage?

None other than the Vacation Bible School drama room.

The story?

The woman with the "issue" of blood.

The actors?

Jesus and I, where the only "issue" that mattered was the one going on within my heart.

In all my decades of doing VBS, no other night has been more profound than this one. Somewhere in the middle of my narrating the drama and acting as the lead participant, God dealt with my heart in pure measure. I'm not sure when the "drama" ended and the personal application took hold, but somehow God managed to weave them together in a profound way so as to make a change in my heart.

Acting the part of the woman with an "issue" of blood, I told the children about my unclean status and poverty of soul. About my shame and embarrassment over a wound that refused to find its healing. About the man named Jesus who was rumored to be a healer—a water walker and a feeder of five thousand. About how I wished for his notice, his touch, his time, and his healing. About the crowds and about a man named Jairus whose needs rated higher than mine. About my diminishing expectations for a miracle as I watched this Jesus pass me by.

Peace in the pardon

He did pass me by, and then I did something I thought I would never have the courage to do.

I reached. I took hold of the hem of his garment. Some call this "him" Preacher Billy. But in that moment, the robe that I held in my hands belonged to Jesus. I gripped tightly, even as the word in the original Greek language, "haptomai," indicates "to fasten oneself to; adhere to, cling to."[2] This was no casual hold. This was a grasping of the divine, believing that with the holding comes healing.

Tears poured down my cheeks as I clung to the hem of my husband's robe. Children were stunned. Some chuckled, perhaps thinking I had played my part to the tee. The older children—those adults who have come to VBS this week to offer their willing participation as chaperones—well, they knew better. They know me better. Kingdom work was at hand. If not in the hearts of the children, then certainly in the heart of this grown woman.

And for a few brief moments, I caught a glimpse of an eternal teaching that is meant for each one of us this day. It comes in the form of a question. A divine invitation for all of God's children to join him in sacred dialogue. . . .

"Who touched me?"

These three simple words hold the answer for our healing. Jesus' question embodies his theology of faith—of believing that what is required for our wholeness resides at the end of our arms. Our grasp.

Our healing from Jesus comes with initiative. With our asking. With our faith-filled approach to the Son of God, even when the current chaos competes for his attention. With our crawling, if need be, to get to his feet. With the thrust of a hand through the tangle of robes, believing that a garment's edge is more than enough to garner the favor and blessing of God.

"Who touched me?"

The "who" in Jesus' question is each one of us. The "me" in the question is him. And the word between the two—*"touched"*—is the bridge that connects all things temporal to the eternal healing of heaven.

We must be willing to reach in order to receive. We must move beyond our tight-fisted clenching and our childish thinking that keeps us on the sidelines self-medicating our wounds because the reach seems too risky. Too vulnerable. Too trusting for an "issue" that has become our constant shadow. Maybe for years. Maybe even for twelve. Perhaps, even for more than we care to number.

We've grown accustomed to our "constant," to the point that we no longer believe in the prospect of change. Our faith is buried deeply beneath our wounds so that when Jesus passes by for the grasping, he rarely garners our notice.

Let it not be so, my friends. Let us never get so caught up in our pain that we fail to see our Jesus when he walks our way. Let's not wait for our faith to be big before we reach. Let's reach now, even in our little. Let's strip away the intrigue and the mystery of our need, and let's take hold of his hem while we can. Even when bloody and barren and broken, let us boldly stretch these arms through the pressing in of the crowds so that we, too, can know the power of a Father's healing touch.

"Who touched me?"

How would you answer? How long has it been since you've activated your faith by stretching forth your hands to take hold of him, even when it was hard and heavy and seemingly hopeless? Your answer to Christ's question embodies your theology of faith. You will never be able to respond to his inquiry until you have actually touched him, tasted him, and held the power of his resurrecting grace as your own.

Being able to answer the question requires a previous action on your part. And with that action, you hold the keys to the kingdom. You hold the living Christ as your own.

I've held him tonight. I want the same for you; thus, I pray—

Give us the strength, Father, for the reach. We struggle with our many issues, and our faith seems small and unwilling to move past our wounding. Come to us, Jesus. Bring your hem close enough for our touch. Tend to our wounds and speak healing to our hurts. And when it feels too hard and the heaviness threatens to keep us in a corner, give us the boldness of our sister from so long ago, who had faith enough to believe and courage enough to grasp. I long for a grasping faith, Lord. Grow me toward this sacred end. Amen.

Peace in the pardon

A further pause . . .

- What are some of the most pressing "issues" facing you in your current season of living?

- Describe the ways that you've chosen to deal with these issues.

- Take time to read the full account of the woman's healing as found in Luke 8:40–53. In what ways are the two accounts of healing similar?

- Many people were crowding in on Jesus that day. Why did Jesus notice her touch more than the others? See verse 46.

- Record Jesus' response to both women in verses 48 and 54.

- Reach through the crowd this day and take hold of your Father's healing. Your "issue" is not too big or too bothersome to receive our Lord's attention. Receive his words of benediction, even as he spoke them to these two women long ago.

 *a spring's visit to a winter's prison*

Then she called, "Samson, the Philistines are upon you!" He awoke from his sleep and thought, "I'll go out as before and shake myself free." But he did not know that the LORD had left him. Then the Philistines seized him, gouged out his eyes and took him down to Gaza. Binding him with bronze shackles, they set him to grinding in the prison. But the hair on his head began to grow again after it had been shaved.

—Judges 16:20–22

There is—
no prison so dank,
no shackle so confining,
no disobedience so egregious,
no blindness so dark,
no winter so long,
so as to keep spring from making its arrival. Its buds and blossoms come regardless of the bleak season preceding its entrance.

Resurrection is the hallowed crescendo after the harrowing silence of a winter's death—a season's stripping that reduces branches to the bare and wide-opened embrace of colder winds. It is hard to think spring when winter continues its insistent knock. It is hard to think grace when the consequences of sin leave a soul chained and blinded with remembrance.

Samson knew something of winter's bite.

His life began well. He ended on the upswing, but the living in between reads more like a tragedy rather than the famed position given him in Hebrews 11, the "Hall of Faith" chapter.

God wanted more for him. His parents planned for more. But for more to be his portion, Samson would have to walk the plans of his God. And for all of the ways that he might have been faithful to those plans and to his covenantal Nazarite vow, we are privy to a majority of his "less than" moments. Moments that included:

- chasing after all manner of foreign women;
- gleaning honey from the carcass of a dead lion and feeding it to his parents;
- exacting revenge via foxtails and torches, the jawbone of a donkey, and the sword of his own hands;

playing games with God's truth rather than honoring God's truth with sacred and in reverent fear.

Indeed, some would argue that Samson earned his chains, his blindness, and his mockery by men. Open rebellion to God's ways always yields a well-deserved humbling at some point. I know I have hosted my fair share of showcase moments along the way.

But to remain stuck in our chains—to assign ourselves a place of permanent shame and penance within the cold and barren of winter—is to delay or altogether miss the promise of spring.

And to miss the grace of spring is to miss everything.

Samson's spring came near his end. If you are one prone to spectacular endings—the grandeur and polish of an epic finish—you'll miss it. Samson's resurrection didn't begin between two pillars (Judges 16:29); it began in the dark and in the depths of a lonely prison cell.

> Then the Philistines seized him, gouged out his eyes and took him down to Gaza. Binding him with bronze shackles, they set him to grinding in the prison. But the hair on his head began to grow again after it had been shaved.
>
> —Judges 16:22

Just in case you missed it, let me type it again.

"The hair on his head began to grow again."

Grow—the verb "samah" in the Hebrew language, meaning, "to grow, to spring forth, to sprout."[3]

No matter Samson's sin and no matter his rebellion, God's promise of spring came to him in his darkest night, the seeds of which would grow and would ultimately result in his finest hour. God visited the cell of a sinner and planted his grace within Samson in a very literal way.

I don't know if Samson thought a lot about his hair in those days; I imagine he did. When a soul is stripped, both spiritually and physically, one cannot help but look for any sign of covering—of hope and rebirth, of new growth and of springing forth. With every passing day and with every difficult grinding, whenever Samson ran his fingers through the sparse seedlings of a new and growing strength, he was reminded of just how far he had fallen and of the grace afforded him for its gradual return.

It did return, at least in part. That's the way of God's grace. Despite our willful choices and hardened rebellion regarding God's plans for our lives, his mercy is ready and available for its return. He planned for grace's arrival, long before our sin mandated its need.

"The days are coming," declares the Lord, "when I will fulfill the gracious promise I made to the house of Israel and to the house of Judah. In those days and at that time I will make a righteous Branch sprout from David's line; he will do what is just and right in the land. In those days Judah will be saved and Jerusalem will live in safety. This is the name by which it will be called: The Lord Our Righteousness."

—Jeremiah 33:14–16

Just in case you missed it, let me type it again.

"In those days and at that time I will make a righteous Branch sprout from David's line."

Sprout—the verb "samah" in the Hebrew language, meaning, "to grow, to spring forth, to sprout."[4]

God's grace—shooting forth and bursting onto the scenes of our lives. Sometimes through a hair's sprouting. All the time through a Son's coming. A Son's dying. A Son's springing forth on a spring morning, announcing once and for all that resurrection is here to stay.

His resurrection is the gift of spring; it follows the stripping and cold of a winter season. A season when remembering God's promises is critical to survival.

There is—

no prison so dank,

no shackle so confining,

no disobedience so egregious,

no blindness so dark,

no winter so long,

so as to keep spring from making its arrival. None. And that, my friends, gets a hallelujah from my spirit and a prayer of thanks from my knees as they hit the bedroom floor in absolute wonder and awe of the gracious grace that has been sown on my behalf. It is growing in strength with every passing day and with every intentional glimpse I make into the treasures of God's Word. He is the worthy pause of my heart this week. Yours too. Thus, I pray—

Grow us, Father, into a deeper understanding of all things eternal. Let us not settle for our prisons; instead, renew our hearts towards a healthier life—one that is free of the chains and the condemnation that seek to keep us captive in sin's remembrance. Spring us forth from our cells, and grow us in the light and truth of spring's renewal—the resurrected life of Easter's gift. In the name of the Father who knows us, and the Son who loves us, and the Holy Spirit who so willingly tends to us, Amen and Amen.

A further pause . . .

- Describe your most recent winter season. What led you there—disobedience, the actions of another, self-induced circumstances?

- In what ways did you know the "stripping" of our Father during that time? In what ways did you know the planting of his sacred grace?

- Take time to review Hebrews 11, giving close attention to those commended for their faith.

- Write your own memorial—how you want to be eulogized alongside the saints of old. By faith, (your name) _____.

- Tell God and believe, by faith, that your "now" as well as your ending will script accordingly.

 *my ashes, God's Spirit*

And we know that in all things God works for the good of those who love him, who have been called according to his purpose.

—Romans 8:28

"God loves ashes, because ashes can be blown anywhere by the wind of his Spirit."

Dr. Steve Seamands' words ring in my heart this night even as they did some thirteen years ago while attending an Ash Wednesday service on the campus of Asbury Theological Seminary. Several of us had gathered during the noon hour in the chapel located on the basement level of the Beeson Center. Students, coworkers, professors, all manner of worshippers came together for the imposition of ashes that would mark the beginning of our pilgrimages to the Easter cross.

I will never forget that day; I will never forget that season.

My season of ashes. It was a time in my life when I was forced to come to some conclusions about my faith, my trust, and my belief in the God I had known all of my life. A season that followed some hard living. Some bad choices. Some sinful strides. Some pitiful results. A time when heartache finally wounded my soul deeply enough and vividly enough so as to wake me out of my dismal dinge and bring me to my knees in humble surrender.

I couldn't trace the hands of God in those days. I only knew them to be present in the lives of those who so willingly shared in my journey. At that time, my walk of faith reflected but a partial knowing—a fragmented glimpse into something greater and bigger and beyond the pain that currently seared my flesh and that scattered the resulting ashes into the wind.

I longed for their safe landing. For God to pick them up with the breath of his Spirit and blow them into everlasting significance. He had a lot to work with, for my ash heap was considerable. My surrender to the flames of his purifying fire had come at no small price. It had cost me dearly; it cost him too.

This is the way of grace. It costs. One doesn't receive it without first needing it. And the need for grace is always preceded by the selfish need to walk in isolation from its grip.

I'd been walking that isolation for a long season, and when the loneliness finally outwore its welcome, I came home. Fully home. Back to the arms of a loving God and with the hope that he could take any portion of my mess and, through his mercy, mold it into something that mattered.

Indeed, I couldn't trace the hands of God in those days; I didn't dare try. I was too humbled and grateful to ask for any further clarification in my many matters. But I can trace them now and see how he was working on my behalf and in my favor.

It's been a long time since that season of ashes. God's grace in my life has been abundant. But every now and then there comes a rich portion of remembrance. A time when the imposition of ashes revisits the scene of my life and requires another walk of surrender to the altar. A time when I cannot see the "end" God has in mind, and I am required to trust him for the conclusion. Having walked this road before, and having witnessed the beauty that often rises from the ashes, my heart is strengthened for the flames of God's sacred fire.

If Dr. Seamands was right; if, in fact, "God loves ashes because ashes can be blown anywhere by the wind of his Spirit," then I pray for his holy fire to be my portion this night. Why? Because God's mighty breath has blown my ashes in some mighty good directions.

In this moment, he's blown me to you. It has taken well over a decade to carry the likes of my mess into the likes of yours. I couldn't see it back then, but I can see it now. And it's good, and it's worthy. And your heart, if you're willing, is one of the places where he intends for a portion of my ashes to land. Truly, you are more than I deserve.

But that is the way of grace. It is the lavish, unmerited expression of a Father's love. God's gift of mercy will always exceed our mess and, when allowed, will turn our ashes into a beautiful witness of kingdom influence. It doesn't make sense; not yet. But there is coming a day when our mirrored understanding will give way to his, and we will know, in full, what we now hold in part.

We will see the tracing of our Father's hands through all of our seasons, ashes and otherwise, and be thankful for the breath that has finally landed them in a safe place of concluding and everlasting significance. Thus, I pray—

Bring me to ashes, Father, and blow me where you will and for your glory. Today, my life doesn't breathe without some questions—some wrestling about the road that lies ahead; thus, I bring them to your altar and ask for your refining of them according to your vision, not mine. Thank you for my brokenness that has brought me to this place of partial understanding. Thank you for the freedom that is mine because of your grace. Thank you for the imposition of your ashes that has cleansed me from mine. Keep me to the cross, to my knees, and to your altar all the days of my life, until my earthly journey ends safely in your kingdom come. Even so, come quickly, Lord Jesus. Amen.

Peace for the Journey

A further pause . . .

- Consider a time in your own life when you couldn't see the tracing of God's hands. As you look back on the situation, can you now see how God was using that season to bring you to where you are today? Explain.

- What questions do you have for God? Questions about your life, your future? How do your past experiences strengthen your faith in God for the current unknowns in your life?

- Please read the following scriptures about God's plans for your future, replacing your doubts with his truth.

    Proverbs 3:5–8

    Jeremiah 29:10–14

    John 14:1–5

    2 Corinthians 5:17–21

    Philippians 1:3–6

    1 Peter 2:9–10

2
Peace in the mirror

Now we see but a poor reflection as in a mirror; then we shall see face to face. Now I know in part; then I shall know fully, even as I am fully known.

—1 Corinthians 13:12

the hope of forced perception

When I was a child, I talked like a child, I thought like a child, I reasoned like a child. When I became a man, I put childish ways behind me. Now we see but a poor reflection as in a mirror; then we shall see face to face. Now I know in part; then I shall know fully, even as I am fully known.
—1 Corinthians 13:11–12

What do you see when you look into a mirror? How do you respond to your reflection? Does your reflection draw your tears?

Mine did, a few days ago while I was sitting in the beauty shop. I didn't expect my tears. They arrived without notice and demanded my full participation. What I expected was a new hairdo to replace the old. What I received instead was an ample cry, some sturdy tissues, and a few moments of tearful confession before a sympathetic stylist and a large mirror.

Mirrors do that—especially big ones. They force perception—an inward look when we are more than content to look elsewhere. For a rare few of us, a mirror's reflection is a comfortable fit. But for me, at least on this occasion, it was a tortuous few moments of self-examination. Accordingly, my tearful surrender to an unsuspecting audience.

She simply asked me if she needed to "cut more." I simply replied with my, "I just feel like I want to cry." And then I did.

Really, it wasn't about the hair. Tears deserve better than the externals we are so quick to assign them. We may think that our tears are based on the rudimentary, on the seen and on the simple, but our external manifestations of "wet" root deeper. They bear witness to the inward prod of a heart's stirring.

My stirring? Well, it took a few moments of tender perception, but in the end, the focus became clear. The reflection of the woman staring back at me was and continues to be a woman who is walking with a restless ache. A woman who is struggling to find herself, to like herself, to see herself beyond the labeling that is so quick to attach. It is a struggle that's been working its way in and out of me for weeks now.

The mirror? Well, it simply heightened the dilemma, bringing my angst into sharp focus.

The easiest thing to do would be to avoid my reflection, to pack away all mirrors in hopes of keeping the ache at bay, just below the surface and hidden enough to pretend that it doesn't exist. Easy is adequate if one is content to stay "as is." But easy doesn't cut it with a person who is intent on the pursuit of holiness.

Peace in the mirror

Mirrors are a crucible for refinement along those lines. They are an expedient tool to increase a pilgrim's progress toward sanctification. But when we tuck them away, when we refuse a deeper probe into the pooled reflection looking back at us, we limit the process of our becoming. Staying "as is" takes the stage, while God's sacred shaping of our hearts and lives takes a seat.

This is child's play, my friends, yet one in which we are often willing to proffer our participation. A game of hide-and-seek, where hiding holds a premium over the seeking, much less the finding. And while it's easier to stay hidden, it's better to be found. Why? Because in the finding we begin in our fragile understanding of what it means to be known, to be loved, and to be trusted with the extravagant grace of a great God. He isn't content to leave us as we are. Rather, he is wholly intent on shaping us into something more.

His.

This is the hope of a mirrored reflection. To look intently into perfection and then to realize that, while we've still so far yet to travel toward that end, we are closer now than we were in the moments prior to our gaze. Albeit a poor reflection, a willing look inward is the seeding of a powerful fruition. Not the end of the process, but rather a good beginning to an up-and-coming grand finish that punctuates into a likeness of Father God.

We won't see it all up front. We'll want to, but to know wholeness, we must be willing to know in part—to vision beyond the shades of gray that dim current focus in order to see the brilliant kaleidoscope that paints a final masterpiece. To hold the pieces of an unfinished puzzle and to call them good and necessary and part of a soon-to-be completed process. To believe beyond the "seen" and to trust that the "unseen" far exceeds our momentary grasp at understanding.

This is the hopeful outcome of a willing gaze into an unobstructed mirror. Forced perception that moves a heart toward perfection isn't a wasted pause, even when that pause lands you in a stylist's chair. God's mirrors are all around us; not to condemn us, but to shape us and to conform us into a better image that breathes with the fingerprints of a Holy Father's intention.

May we all have the courage to step up, to gaze inward, and then to begin in our understanding of what it means to hold forever in our reflection. Thus, I pray—

Bring us to our mirrors and to our surrender of the reflected truth, Father. Let the initial shock of what we see be replaced by your holy possibility. Let not the trappings of our flesh keep us from visioning what you would have us become—a people wrapped in your likeness and moving on toward final perfection. Forgive us for the labels that we place upon ourselves and others; brand us with the only label that bears lasting significance—a name that reads "holy, consecrated as unto the Lord." Move me to that place of sacred consecration and the forced perception required to keep me there. It is a privilege to wear your name. May the mirrors in my life always host your reflection within mine. Amen.

A further pause . . .

- Take some time this day to linger with your Father before a mirror. Don't rush your time of reflection. Record what you see, both outwardly and inwardly.

- What areas of your life need some fine-tuning as a result of your forced perception?

- Why is forced perception sometimes a difficult obedience?

- The apostle Peter understood the pause of forced perception. Take time to read about his struggle before the mirror as found in the following two Scripture passages: John 18:15–27 and John 21:1–19. Describe the events that forced Peter's look inward. How did Father God gently restore Peter's reflection? What was the outcome of Peter's willing pause? See Matthew 16:17–19.

Your reflection in the mirror can birth the same. Go forth this day, believing that you hold the keys to the kingdom of God within your heart! That is the hopeful expectation of a mirror's pause.

God's plow, my longing

He said to another man, "Follow me." But the man replied, "Lord, first let me go and bury my father." Jesus said to him, "Let the dead bury their own dead, but you go and proclaim the kingdom of God." Still another man said, "I will follow you, Lord; but first let me go back and say good-by to my family." Jesus replied, "No one who puts his hand to the plow and looks back is fit for service in the kingdom of God."

—Luke 9:59–62

There is a difficult tug that exists within my heart—a pull between my love for the plow and my longing for a backward glance. A sacred tension exists between the two, because God has seeded my temporal flesh with the capacity to focus in both directions—forward and reverse. Thus, the rub.

As Christians, we are charged with the task of understanding and overcoming the strain between these extremes. We are made to plow, yet we are prone to a backward glance. And somewhere in the midst of our understanding the difference between the two, we must surrender our fleshly tendencies in order to undertake the higher cause of Jesus Christ. If we refuse the learning, we are useless before God and in his service for the greater good of humanity.

There is a new song out on music radio; I liked it the first time I heard it. But after a further examination of its lyrics, I determined it to be incompatible with my life of faith. Not because I am bound by legalism, but rather because it tugged at something deeper within me.

A backward glance. A life I no longer live, and yet a life that pulls me toward swift surrender. Sometimes through a song. Sometimes through all manner of triggers that call for my retreat. And because I am not in the business of retreating from God's calling upon my life, I must refuse the invitation. God's Spirit enables me to refuse; but when I neglect his promptings, when I choose a backward glance over the plow that grips my heart, I lose a portion of the holy ground that is mine to claim for God's kingdom agenda.

A cluttered mind filled with a backward longing is a mind unfit to move on with God. Jesus said as much when speaking to a few well-meaning pilgrims who intended to join his cause but refused his calling. At first glance, it is a difficult teaching to understand. Jesus' words seem harsh; it seems that these men simply wanted to bring some closure to their past before moving on with Jesus in their present. But Christ calls into question their motives and their usability within his kingdom purposes:

> No one who puts his hand to the plow and looks back is fit for service in the kingdom of God.
>
> —Luke 9:62

What a reproof! What a rejection. It is warranted, but the reason for Christ's stern rebuke is often missed because of our focus on the painful severity of his response.

The culprit for his reprimand? Four seemingly harmless words spoken by both men, yet when placed in context alongside the Savior's sacred call for discipleship, words that breathed as offensive and, therefore, worthy of a harsh reproach: "Lord, first let me . . ." (Luke 9:59, 61).

"Lord" and "first let me" is an unholy coupling. My firsts and the Lord's firsts are incompatible. We cannot claim him as Lord and still harbor a "me first" within. We can try. In fact, we have mastered the vernacular. We simply cloak our "me firsts" in less obvious and less offensive terms.

We don't always mean to—not always. But on each occasion when our minds trade in the plow of God's "right now" for the pull of a backward glance, we offend the cause for which he died. We limit our holy usefulness because our "me firsts" take the lead. And when it comes to the gospel of Jesus Christ and the seeding of it within the soil given to us for the plowing, his leading takes a back seat to no one. No thing. No memory. No backward glance.

When God calls, if our response is anything but a resounding "yes," then we remain shackled to a past that breathes without hope and within the boundaries of an irreversible history that has already been written.

I don't know about you, but I don't want to be stuck in my history. I don't want to miss God's "ahead" because of the "me first" of my "behind." Honestly, I can't think of one moment in my yesterdays that is worthy of sacrificing one moment of my now with Jesus. Can you? If you can, may I be so bold as to suggest that you are going nowhere with God?

You're stuck, and being stuck isn't an excuse for staying as you are. You are a sinner saved by grace who is given the high and holy privilege of moving onto perfection. It is within your power to do so, because if you are a Christian, you house the presence and the living power of God's Spirit within.

There is no mystery to your moving forward. It simply requires your refusal to longingly entreat the pull of a backward glance. Backward glances come in all shapes and sizes. Regardless of the triggers, if allowed safe sanctuary within your mind and your heart, their voices will be heard.

It sounds a lot like "me first," which looks a lot like refusal. Whenever we refuse God's invitation to follow, his voice will be heard. It is louder than ours and cuts with more clarified precision than any justification we can offer in the matter. And that, my friends, sounds a whole lot like holy rejection—a painful contrast to what I truly and deeply desire.

I want to be fit for kingdom purpose. I want the privilege of sacred participation in the higher cause of Jesus Christ. I want the same for you. Thus, I pray—

Purify and cleanse our minds, Lord. Purge and eradicate the "me firsts" from our wills. Let your plow be our portion and the pull of a backward glance be our refusal. Fill us to the outer edges of our flesh with the wild and untamed overflow of your Spirit. You are our future. You are our forever. Keep our eyes fixed accordingly. Amen.

A further pause . . .

- When was the last time you felt the pull of a backward glance? Describe.

- Identify some of the "triggers" that often take you there.

- How is "Lord" and "first let me" an incompatible coupling?

- What do the following scriptures have to say about putting our hearts and hands to "God's plow"?

    Matthew 10:37–39

    Matthew 16:21–26

    Philippians 3:7–14

sacred mystery, intended ministry

I know that nothing good lives in me, that is, in my sinful nature. For I have the desire to do what is good, but I cannot carry it out. For what I do is not the good I want to do; no, the evil I do not want to do—this I keep on doing. Now if I do what I do not want to do, it is no longer I who do it, but it is sin living in me that does it. . . . What a wretched man I am! Who will rescue me from this body of death? Thanks be to God—through Jesus Christ our Lord!

—Romans 7:18–20; 24–25

I've heard it said that "silence is golden." Perhaps. But what about those times when silence speaks otherwise? When silence is used as a weapon rather than as an avenue for avoiding conflict?

I hurt someone recently. Not with my words but with my silence. I'm prone to both techniques. One speaks louder, more penetrating, and more "in the moment." The other speaks softer, yet almost always inflicts a harsher wound that lasts longer, festers deeper, and in the end, requires a harder humbling. This has been my recent experience; the situation that could have easily been resolved months ago has been nurtured and tended to by my silence.

Yesterday I broke my silence. I confronted the situation involving a member of the body of Christ and humbly asked for forgiveness. I do not relish these moments—times when my flesh and faith war against one another and I am forced to battle the thing through to resolution. My flesh said "no." My faith shouted otherwise. I have lived with God long enough to know when his Spirit is prompting me to a further examination of myself—a deeper look into the mirror, where the reflection staring back at me isn't always so perfect and pretty.

Rarely have I lived picture perfectly. There have been lovely moments—moments that capture a portrait of true intimacy between Father and child. All too often, though, those moments are accompanied by occasions of pitiful sin, when all I can do is cry out to God about the wretched condition of my heart.

And while private confession to God secures eternal forgiveness, there are times when a further step of obedience is required. There are times that include confession to another, where temporary relief is contingent upon the offended party's willingness to extend grace. And therein lies the rub—the one reason why some sins in our lives never know resolution, why lines are drawn and friendships are broken and wounded pilgrims retreat to loneliness rather than risk relationships.

Making things right with another is a hard portion of Christian obedience, and yet, it is one we must embrace if we are to move beyond the boundaries of spiritual infancy. We are meant for solid food and for maturity—for being built up into a spiritual household where the bricks of our lives are aligned alongside the lives of our brothers and sisters, including those we have wounded along the way and those who have returned the favor.

It is a divine mystery, this ministry of forgiveness and reconciliation. Christ wrote the manual, and we have spent the better part of two thousand years trying to piece together the sacred clues about how to wash another's feet. How to love our enemies. How to turn the other cheek. How to humble the heart and bend the knee to ask for grace and in equal measure to dispense that grace. How to serve the body of Christ unconditionally and live in unified purpose.

Feeble in our flesh, and with partial understanding, we undertake our role as Christ's ambassadors. Rarely is the outcome perfect. Still and yet, we wash. We love. We turn. We bend, and we bow. We serve, and we live with the hope that the outcome merits a divine "well done" from the Savior who shepherds our growth and is pleased with our obedience to his staff and rod.

This divine mystery is a pivotal key to personal holiness. I desire to be the consecrated work of Jesus Christ. I don't want to linger at the edge of *almost*. *Almost* pure. *Almost* clean. *Almost* mirroring a 1 Corinthians 13 kind of love to others. Instead, I want to fully participate in the divine nature as promised to me in God's Word.

> His divine power has given us everything we need for life and godliness through our knowledge of him who called us by his own glory and goodness. Through these he has given us his very great and precious promises, so that through them you may participate in the divine nature and escape the corruption in the world caused by evil desires.
>
> —2 Peter 1:3–4

Simply put, I want to be like Christ. And because of this desire, coupled with the enabling power of God's Spirit living within me, I am able to bend my will to embrace a difficult obedience when he tells me something more is required from me. I did so yesterday.

I cannot predict the outcome of that humbling. What remains to be belongs to God. In obedience, I broke my silence and pled my case for forgiveness. It wasn't easy, but it was right. It was good. It was a portion of holiness, as holiness was meant to be hammered out on the anvil of God's will. Peace has arrived, and God's grace has painted a new reflection in my mirror. Far from perfect, friends, but moving on toward a perfect end.

Some days it's exhausting being a Christian. Some days it feels like a slow death. I think, perhaps, this is what my Father has been after all along. It may take a lifetime to put to death the misdeeds of this body, but to make it home to Jesus as a completed work? Well, for that I'll take a humbling every time. On the other side of such obedience is life with concluding understanding and, finally, freedom from the flesh. Indeed, I think that this is what my Father has been after all along. Thus, I pray—

Bend me, Lord, as you will. Not because I like it, but because I cannot live the life that you have intended for me without it. Exhaust me, Lord, until you rid this flesh of the deeds that so easily entangle me and the sin that keeps me separated from you. Whatever it takes, Lord, wean me from the bottle of spiritual infancy and transform me into your mighty ambassador of reconciliation. You have trusted me with much. Forgive me when I trust you for so little. Transform my personal preferences toward your holy will and use me for your kingdom purposes. Reconcile any portion of your world through me, Lord. Humbly, I receive this ministry—this mystery. Amen.

A further pause . . .

- Consider an occasion when God required you to do the "hard thing" of admitting your wrong to another. Describe. What made it difficult? What was the outcome?

- Owning our sin in private is one thing. Owning it publicly is quite another. Why might this be?

- Consider the repentant heart of the prodigal son. Please read Luke 15:11–24. Describe in detail the son's response when his heart was repentant. Describe the father's heart after hearing his son's confession.

- This is a picture of how forgiveness should work between believers. Unfortunately, it's the exception rather than the rule. What makes forgiveness real? Why do we struggle so freely with that "real"? In other words, what keeps us from modeling true forgiveness with one another?

Peace in the mirror

 pressing in

Not that I have already obtained all this, or have already been made perfect, but I press on to take hold of that for which Christ Jesus took hold of me. Brothers I do not consider myself yet to have taken hold of it. But one thing I do: Forgetting what is behind and straining toward what is ahead, I press on toward the goal to win the prize for which God has called me heavenward in Christ Jesus.
—Philippians 3:12–14

There is a seventh member in our family—a truck that has been with us for more than fifteen years, passed down through the hands of a father to his son, to his daughter, to her son, and then to another one of her sons. Four generations of a family have sat behind the wheel of this '93 Chevy pick-up truck.

The world would level its worth as little more than scrap metal—old and washed up and one step away from a junkyard's grave. But to my family, well, we level its worth a bit higher. Not because of its beauty, but rather because of its bloodlines. This truck originated with my Grandpa Al. He drove it a year before he passed away. My father then took ownership of it for several years until my eldest son was eligible to drive. It seemed reasonable that he be allowed this "junker" to serve as his training ground for better rides down the road. It did, and has now been passed on to his younger brother, who has given our treasured piece of family history a good and steady workout. Through all generations, the truck has been faithful to render its services whenever and wherever needed.

So what do you do with this faithful servant that's been driven hard, regularly neglected, taken for granted, and looked upon with little regard until finally an accident causes its bumper to be pried away from the frame?

What do you do with a fifteen-year-old vehicle that's logged more than 100,000 miles, that no longer hosts a working air-conditioner, and that hardly seems worthy of an expensive repair, especially when other needs are pressing heavily upon an already dwindling bank account? I'll tell you what you do. You press its need into an old, faithful tree—one that can absorb the shock and that can realign the bumper back alongside its original frame. That is what we did.

The outcome? Well, not picture perfect, but the tree coupled with the willing obedience to "press in" has yielded a drivable vehicle that will service this family for a season longer, perhaps even a generation somewhere down the road.

As it is with our family truck, so it is with me. Perhaps, even with you.

What do we do when our frames begin to show the wear of a hard drive? A regular neglect? A taking for granted? A little regard for regular maintenance?

What do we do when an accident pries our hearts away from the original frame—the Author of our frames? How do we respond when we know that a heart's servicing is necessary, but when the bank account is empty and incapable of such a transaction?

I tell you what I do. I press my need into an old, faithful tree—one that absorbed the shock on my behalf over two thousand years ago and is more than capable of my realignment every time that I am willing to be pressed into necessary obedience.

It may not yield a full perfection at this time. But it's coming. If not here, then there. And in the time lived in between the two, I will continue to press in and press on to take hold of everything for which Christ Jesus has taken hold of me. I am not sure what my "everything" looks like; in fact, I am fairly confident that God intends for much of it to remain veiled. Why?

Because that which remains unseen is that which grows my faith.

When I cannot see beyond the fog that surrounds me, a "pressing in" is required. When my plans cannot be managed or manipulated by my well-intentioned will, God presses the issue by urging me toward an intentional pause and by asking me to trust him with a fast from the world's noisy insistence.

There is strength to be found in the silence of a tree's press. Never is it absent or unavailable to us. But there are times when we are absent and unavailable. In part because priorities get derailed. But mostly because we are willing to trade in the sweet sound of our Father's voice for the resounding gongs and clanging cymbals of the world's shout. Sometimes it takes a fast to recognize the difference. By pressing into God's tree, we are better able to witness the profound extreme between the two—God's song and the world's attempt at imitation. The difference is staggering, and I am no longer willing to make that trade.

I don't know how your truck is driving this week, but if you are feeling a bit old and worn and pried away from your sacred frame, let my lesson be yours. If God is urging you toward an intentional pause, press into his tree and then press in some more until he realigns your heart with his. He can absorb your pain; this has always been the intention of the Calvary tree that he planted on your behalf more than two thousand years ago.

Press in, child of God, and press on. Move on and take hold of all of that for which Christ Jesus has taken hold of you—a glorious perfection. Yours and mine. Thus, I pray—

Peace in the mirror

Pause me in silence, Father, each and every day for the sweet revelation of your voice. When I allow the world's noise to drown out your melody, shut me down and bring me to my surrender at the foot of your cross. Strengthen my frame for holy submission, and press into my flesh the splintered reminder of the price that you paid for my realignment. May I never lose the wonder of your cross and the glorious participation of your presence in my life. So be it. Amen.

A further pause . . .

- Take some time to consider how your "truck" has been driving in recent days. Describe.

- When you experience the weariness of a long and hard drive, what steps do you usually take to recover from the ride?

- Read the following scriptures and record the ways in which our "pressing in" to God always proves to be the right move:

2 Samuel 22:31–37

Psalm 46:1–4

Psalm 91:1–4

Matthew 11:28–29

crossroads

*This is what the L*ORD *says: "Stand at the crossroads and look; ask for the ancient paths, ask where the good way is, and walk in it, and you will find rest for your souls. But you said, 'We will not walk in it.'"*

—Jeremiah 6:16

"If you write conviction, Elaine, you'd better live conviction or else be prepared for conviction to find its way to your table."

This was God's message to me in my spirit moments ago. It came fast and certain and with resolute clarity. I kept repeating it for fear that I would forget it before finding my pen. It happens sometimes. God impresses his thoughts upon my heart, and I cannot help but give them ample room to grow—to breathe their depth as I take the time to unpack them before God and his Word.

Tonight I unpack them alongside the prophet Jeremiah's pen as he scripted God's heart to a people who had lost their way. He instructed them to stand at the crossroads and examine the path before them and behind them, to the left and to the right of them, and then to ask God for his directional good—those ancient paths that secured safe passage to his place of rest.

His heart.

It would have been easy for them to find their way home if they had been willing to stand at the crossroads. But they weren't; they didn't; and consequently, they found themselves on the road toward a restless exile and a formidable captivity. Nothing good and certainly no rest came for those who were adamantly opposed to a pause at God's crossroads.

We all come to a crossroads at least once in our lives. Some of us, multiple times. Whether we are aware of the depth of the pause or not, we are quick to mouth its refrain. *I'm standing at a crossroads, and I don't know what to do. Where to turn. What path to take. What wisdom to choose.*

I understand. I've said as much even this day. But there is a danger in our paying lip service to our crossroads. As God's children, dearly loved and carefully protected, when we come to a crossroads in our journey, he asks more of us than simply an approach to the process. He means for us to fully engage with its truth. To come to the center of the matter, where beam meets beam. Where horizontal hammers into vertical. Where wood and nails collide. Where faith and flesh intersect to bleed in sacred juncture.

When we do that—when we stand in the middle of Christ's crossroads at Calvary—it is easy to discern the good and ancient path that will secure us safe passage to God's rest. When we center our lives at the heart of his willing sacrifice, no matter the direction we turn—whether before or behind, to the left or to the right—we are bathed in the lavish cover of a Father's love. We are reminded of just how far he traveled on our behalf so that we, like the ancients of old, can find our way home.

Unfortunately, many of us never make it that far. We choose the perimeter of the cross because, quite frankly, the center bleeds too red, too messy, and too fully. We deem our standing "at" the cross with Jesus as enough; but God calls each one of us to something greater.

He asks for us to stand "in" the crossroads with him.

Then, and only then, will we be able to measure the worth of God's intended rest and peace for our lives. It is a peace I want for always. My heart's desire is to walk the path of the ancients and to rest in God's goodness as I go. Thus, I write the conviction of my heart. I am prepared to live its depth so that conviction doesn't revisit my lip service with the poke and prod of a Father's hurt.

Today I am willing to walk to Calvary because I feel deeply in need of doing so. In many ways, I seem to be standing at a crossroads. There are decisions to be made. Big ones. Ones that not only involve my future, but also ones that include the futures of those whom I dearly love.

Rather than stand at the perimeter of the cross, I'm going into its center in order to stand where Christ has stood and to receive the cleansing truth of my salvation. I believe that my vision will be clearer there, that wisdom will be more readily available, and that the path of the ancients will present itself so that I might walk in it and receive God's good and needful rest.

Perhaps, like me, you are sensing the need to walk your heart toward a deeper point of surrender. Your life is at a crossroads, and the only thing you are certain of is your uncertainty about what lies ahead. Would you join me on the road as we walk the beams of our Savior's sacrifice, until we come to the heart of the matter? Would you, this day, be willing to live your convictions all the way into the center of his sacrifice? If so, then the prayer of my heart belongs to you as well. Thus, I pray—

> *Father, your cross is serious business. Forgive me for thinking that I can stand at a distance and see clearly the path you would have me follow. Thank you for the conviction that leads me into the center of your surrender and that washes me in the truth of your love. Baptize my feeble understanding with your wisdom that bleeds pure and true and full of insight so that I can find my way through the chaos that is pressing in ever so tightly. Bring me to your crossroads in my many matters, and show me the path of the ancients. Keep me, then, to the secure path until I find my way to your heart and to your promised rest for my journey. You are my life's end. Bring me safely to my perfected conclusion. Amen.*

A further pause . . .

- Describe a crossroads that you have navigated in your own life. What helped you in making the decision about how to proceed? What was the outcome?

- Consider a time when you stood at the perimeter of Christ's cross and made an important decision regarding your future without the benefit of his input. What was the outcome of that decision?

- Why is it sometimes easier to stand at the perimeter of the cross and "look" rather than stand in the center of its truth and perceive God's path?

- *"If you write conviction, you'd better live conviction or else be prepared for conviction to find its way to your table."* What does this statement mean to you, and when have you known this to be true in your own life?

- Christ lived his spoken/written convictions all the way through to the center of the cross. There was nothing false or contrived about his life. Think of some occasions in Scripture when Christ "spoke" conviction and, therefore, lived it. Record.

3
Peace in the desert

In a desert land he found him, in a barren and howling waste. He shielded him and cared for him; he guarded him as the apple of his eye.

—Deuteronomy 32:10

a call to the desert

So Moses took his wife and sons, put them on a donkey and started back to Egypt. And he took the staff of God in his hand.

—Exodus 4:20

A call to the desert. A God-ordained "sending forth" that requires a hard obedience amidst the hot sand's embrace.

When was the last time you were offered such an invitation?

Sometimes, our pilgrimage in the desert is but a walk-through—a momentary bridge that links our pasts to our futures. A necessary portion of surrender, allowing us to get from where we have been to where we are going.

Sometimes, our pilgrimage in the desert lasts a bit longer—an overnight stay that frequently turns into a season of nights and days with little relief in sight. A longer obedience that allows us the sacred discipline and teaching from the desert sands.

Regardless of its purpose, whether a bridge to what lies ahead or a classroom for the present, a desert's landscape will occasionally be our required portion. Why? Because God better understands the worth behind a desert's pause. The desert has the capacity to shape our Christian character in a way that other venues don't allow. Deserts are sometimes the walk that God allows us because:

- deserts require;
- deserts remind;
- deserts reveal;
- deserts renew.

Some of the best work we will ever do with God will be fleshed out upon the sands of a heated obedience. It would be nice if we could forego the hot and hard of a desert teaching, but our Father understands our propensity for the cool and easy of a *less than* learning. And quite frankly, a *less than* living doesn't fit with a people ordained for the promise of heaven.

God's not after our simply "muddling through" this life; he's after our perfection. One step after another until we fully walk in the fullness of his presence. And to be fully filled with God, we must be fully willing to pilgrim with him, wherever he leads.

For Moses, that meant a desert road to Egypt—a familiar road he had fearfully traveled on his way out of Egypt, with the sole intention of staying hidden. This time, he would walk it with a different intention in mind—perhaps accompanied by his fear, but with the determined purpose of rescuing a people, even if it meant exposing his past.

Moses didn't intend for a heated desert's walk to be his final portion. He intended for his pilgrimage to walk-through—to serve as his bridge from his now to his next. He couldn't have known that its embrace would linger a season longer, forty years longer. If he had, I wonder if his choice to obey would have leveled differently.

He might have chosen to remain as an anonymous sheep-tender of another man's flock instead of tending to God's wild and reckless flock. In doing so—in choosing hiddenness over obedience—Moses would have missed out on something far greater and far more profound than the deliverance of an obstinate and stiff-necked people. He would have missed out on his own deliverance.

God only has one purpose in mind when he sends his children into the desert. Deliverance—both at the corporate and personal level.

This has always been God's way, and lest we think the Israelites were the only captives in need of rescue, we need to look no further than a papyrus basket tangled within the reeds of the Nile to know that God was after more than a nation's deliverance. He was also after the liberation of the one—a fine child named Moses, who had spent his entire life hiding from the certainty of his true identity.

If Moses had foregone the desert, he would have missed out on knowing God at the deepest level. Theirs was a relationship birthed within the arid sands of a difficult submission—both in the coming and going on a desert road and in the life lived between the two.

And while Moses would never live the joy of a peaceful rest in the Promised Land, he would carry the hope of the Promise-Keeper within his heart. For most of us, this kind of theology doesn't match up with our plans for abundant living. We want to live in promise without walking the necessary desert to get there. We want the riches of an easy life without the poverty of a difficult journey. We want renewal without the painful prod of:

- a desert's requirement;
- a desert's reminding;
- a desert's revealing.

I understand. I am prone to similar wants. But I desire something greater—something that exceeds my temporary wants on this side of eternity. I want a relationship with God that boasts the deep intimacy of Moses' kind of knowing.

I think it is fair to say that the intimacy that God and Moses shared wouldn't have run as deep had the desert been missed. It didn't always paint prettily—this relationship between man and his Creator—but in the end, it painted with perfection. It ended with a Father burying the bones of his child in the place of his choosing and with the promise of abundant living brimming on the horizon for a nation and for a fine saint named Moses.

The deliverance of people. The deliverance of one.

This ancient story breathes with the glorious witness for the desert road that is often our necessary requirement. We can walk the desert with hope; not for eventual release, but rather for the promised presence of the One who will abide the journey with us as we go. And for that kind of holy intimacy, I am willing to pilgrim any road that will bring me to such a perfect and completed end. Deliverance. Yours and mine. Thus, I pray—

> *Keep us to the road of our perfection, Lord. Let us not shrink from the desert's heat, but rather let us reason its worth in the light of your promised abiding as we go. Thank you for the path that is best suited to foster our deep intimacy with one another. And when it gets too hot, Father, too hard and too depleting, fill my cup with the ladling waters from your well and with the truth that my journey was meant to step as you have so ordained. Amen.*

Peace in the desert

A further pause . . .

- Consider your most recent desert road. Would you consider it a "walk-through" or a seasonal stop? Describe.

- Walk through your experience with these questions in mind:

    What has the desert "required" of you?

    What has the desert "reminded" you about?

    What has the desert "revealed" about you?

    What has the desert "renewed" in you?

- How have you responded to God's call for deeper intimacy while on the road?

- To walk away from a desert road unchanged is to miss an opportunity for deeper intimacy with God. The next time he presents you a desert's invitation, ponder the eternal possibilities of your participation before refusing your involvement.

a crossroads in the desert

> *The angel of the LORD found Hagar near a spring in the desert; it was the spring that is beside the road to Shur. And he said, "Where have you come from, and where are you going?" "I'm running away from my mistress Sarai," she answered.*
>
> —Genesis 16:7–8

Shur. A desert dwelling on the northeastern border of Egypt. A word meaning "wall" or "fortress."

Fitting that a "wall" be found in a desert. Deserts seem an adequate housing for the bricks and mortar of an aimless wandering. They host them in abundance. Walls of . . .

- desperation;
- hopelessness;
- confinement;
- confusion;
- fear;
- tears.

Walls like these aren't an easy leap. Most often, they refuse movement in any direction. Getting through them requires a deliberate pause for a deliberate question from a deliberate God . . .

"Where have you come from, and where are you going?"

Regardless of the reasons for a desert pilgrimage, there always comes a moment of clarity. A crossroads that requires a halt. A brick wall that demands a breather. A crisis of faith that necessitates an answer. It may take days to arrive at that moment. It may take years; but when you do, your response to God's question embodies your perspective for your journey—your walk from your "now" to your "next."

Hagar would have her moment of clarity. It wasn't conceived in eloquence. Desert clarity rarely is. Instead, it was birthed through a series of selfish choices made on her behalf by a couple who walked their own desert of desperation—barrenness.

Barrenness seems to work that way. If not tended to by the heart and hands of a loving Father, emptiness in an individual—in this case two individuals—almost always breeds emptiness in another. Deserts are welcoming places for the exponential growth of the desperate.

Hagar walked her pregnant desperation in isolation—without income, without family, without love, and without a spiritual heritage that included a covenantal God. Her "fear and her frantic" framed the choices of her feet. Faith would have been the best option, but her heritage as an Egyptian slave hadn't allowed her that leap. Not yet. Thus, Hagar headed for the desert. The desert welcomed her distraction and gave her ample room to deliberate her diminishing options.

There is always space enough to ponder in a desert. For all its ills and aches and required steps of heated obedience, the desert breathes with an open landscape big enough to house our contemplations. And when we come to our Shur—to the wall in our many matters—God is waiting for us, even as he was waiting for Hagar.

She came with multiple questions. He came with two: "Where have you come from, and where are you going?"

He knew the answers before he asked, but with the asking, Hagar was forced to grapple with the uncertainties that drove her to this one moment of clarity. Where she came from was a life lived within the community of a people on the road to promise—a life confined by a covenant that she could not claim. Where she was going was back to a life lived on the road to Shur—a life confined by the walls of a desert. For Hagar, both roads ended with captivity—with walls that could not be climbed but only surrendered to in desperation for the lesser of two perceived "evils."

Behind her? Someone else's promise. Ahead of her? Shur. A straight line between two very confining choices, or so it seemed. But God offered Hagar another choice that day. He offered it to her through a third, unspoken question that links the past with the future. A question that, when filtered through the heart of a Father, would lead Hagar to willingly embrace a change of course.

Not, "Where have you come from, and where are you going?" but rather, "Where are you in this moment, right now?"

Where she was, was in the presence of Covenant Father—the God of the Israelites, who lives to be the God of all people. The God who seeks his children, regardless of their family bloodlines or their traveled terrain. God came to Hagar's desert wall, even as he comes to ours, to reveal the truth of who he is. In doing so, he shatters the foundations of a weary wanting and a weathered unbelief.

Hagar had her moment of clarity. She stood at the crossroads between her past and her future, and for the first time, she noticed her present. His name is Yahweh. She gave him the name *El Roi,* meaning "well of the Living One who sees me."[5] God would speak his own covenant of blessing over Hagar that day, thus allowing her the strength and perspective to return home with a promise she could now claim. No confinement would shadow her steps this time, for she had seen God; and when God is seen, chains are broken. Walls begin to crumble, and promise becomes the sure freedom that trumps the Shur walls of captivity.

Perhaps, like Hagar, you have come to the crossroads in your desert this day. Your moment of clarity stands on the threshold.

Behind you? Someone else's Promised Land. Someone else's possibilities. Someone else's faith. Someone else's confinement. Someone else's need that has saddled you with the pregnancy of someone else's wrong. You are alone, without love, and without a God to call your own.

Ahead of you? Shur. A brick wall that leaves you with little wiggle room and with even fewer options. You bear the scars of that wall because your will has forced the issue. Moment after moment, day after day, season after season, until the blood no longer pours and is replaced by numbed confusion, where the only thing "sure" about Shur is your continuing confinement.

In front of you? Your present. Your best option. Your Jesus and your God who has come to the wall on your behalf and has seen you—has witnessed your need and your desperation and is willing to speak his promise into your hopelessness and his freedom into your captivity.

"Where are you in this moment, right now?"

The desert is big enough to house your contemplation. The desert is big enough to house your God. And somewhere in between the two—your contemplation and your God—there is a clarity waiting to be birthed. It will chart your course home and will gladden your heart with gratitude for the discovery found in the desert's detour. Thus, I pray—

Lead on O King Eternal, to the promise of a desert's journey. Bring me to my Shur—to the wall in my many matters—that will force my pause and my contemplation of you. It matters not how I got here; what matters is that I find you while walking the heat of this difficult obedience. Thank you for seeing me, Father, even as you did your servant Hagar all those years ago. You are faithful to your name, and your eyes are ever on me. When I am prone to my wandering, Lord, remind me of your watchful gaze. How I long to keep in step with you. Amen.

A further pause . . .

- Answer the following questions of God as it pertains to your current situation and your faith.

    Where have you come from?

    Where are you going?

    Where are you in this moment, right now?

- Identify any areas in your life where you need God's clarity.

- Read the following scriptures and claim the promise of "El Roi: The God who sees me."

    2 Chronicles 16:9

    Psalm 33:13–19

    Psalm 121

    Psalm 139:1–16

a turn toward the better
(part one)

> *Then Moses climbed Mount Nebo from the plains of Moab to the top of Pisgah, across from Jericho. There the LORD showed him the whole land. . . . Then the LORD said to him, "This is the land I promised on oath to Abraham, Isaac and Jacob when I said, 'I will give it to your descendants.' I have let you see it with your eyes, but you will not cross over into it." And Moses the servant of the LORD died there in Moab, as the LORD had said.*
>
> —Deuteronomy 34:1, 4–5

Life hasn't turned out the way I thought it would. I thought it would turn toward all things lovely. Instead, it turned differently. Sometimes lovely, sometimes not so much, but never quite in the direction that I thought it would. I feel the profundity of it today as I lie upon my prayer quilt and hammer out my thoughts with God.

He understands. We've been here before. Perhaps, he, too, shares in my disappointment. Not because his love for me breathes less as a result of my sin, but simply because he knows my life could have been different. A better different, but it hasn't.

And this has been his surrendered gift to me—a gift that allows a life to walk within the parameters of a freely chosen will. Mine, not his. I've taken God up on his offer many times. Too many to count. Too awfully painful to chronicle in this moment. I don't tell you this to warrant your sympathy. I simply offer it to you as my explanation for a life that currently lives differently than how I imagined it would live all those many years ago. A time when life walked young and free and full of ideals that had room enough to breathe and the ample innocence to fuel their imagining.

That was then. This is now. And the life lived between innocence's conception and innocence's death was a vast territory of wild and reckless exploration that weeps its remembrance this day.

There are portions of the Promised Land that I will never walk on this side of eternity. Not because my Father doesn't delight in giving me his grace-filled abundance, but rather because my sin has kept me from it. Forty-three years of living have authored some seasons of regrets—times in life that have been lost to the indulgence of fleshly appetites over the reasoned pursuit of holiness.

I understand this. I accept it. I know and live the ramifications of my choices every day. This doesn't mean that life is a pitiful existence for me; it would be a quick leap to live within that conclusion. No, what it means is that life pulses with a full awareness that some of the dreams birthed on the front-end of my existence will find their completed rest only on the backside of eternity. Not here. Not yet, but in the Promised Land that lies just beyond these years of my desert pilgrimage.

Moses walked the territory between a promise given and its final fruition. He never tasted the milk and honey of a God-given dream, much less walked upon its soil. He only witnessed it from atop a mountain, where God opened his eyes to the wild imaginings of sacred possibility. Moses didn't come to the mountain with the hope of God changing his mind in the matter. He'd walked with his Father long enough to reason better.

No, when Moses made the climb up Mt. Nebo that day, he did so knowing that death awaited his arrival. Moses came to the mountain to die. To witness with his eyes a final taste of earth's best and then to witness through life's surrender his first taste of eternity's forever—a lasting best that far exceeds any joy we could walk on this side of heaven.

Indeed, Moses' life hadn't turned out the way he thought it would. His sin kept him from walking God's perfect and best will. But his finish? Well, it turned out better than he ever could have imagined. It turned out perfect and lovely and full of the wild imaginings that had followed him from his youth. . . .

The Promised Land—forever beneath his feet.

It is the same for us, even if life isn't unfolding the way we thought that it would. There is a better day coming, when all of this will be left behind and traded in for something far more wonderful than our minds and hearts can currently conceive.

You may have a hard time making that leap of faith. You may be convinced that your "current" is as good as it gets and that it will live as similar in your "next." May I be so bold as to suggest that you've placed your faith in the wrong king?

This isn't it, oh sleepy pilgrim. What you and I are living today isn't the final word on our forever. This life isn't perfectly lovely, and it certainly isn't God's final best. If I believed this, I would walk away in an instant and pay homage to the closest golden calf, because, quite frankly, this faith walk has been hard fought, painfully lived, and deserves a final promise that exceeds my mind's capacity for imagining.

If I could take hold of everything that God intends for me in my "now," if I could capture the true pulse of a perfected good within my heart and on this side of eternity, then I'm pretty sure that I would stop trying to get there. My pressing on would seem in vain. If this is as good as it gets, then I'm done, because life has not turned in the direction that I thought it would.

But it will, even as it did for Moses. And for all of the sins that have kept me from the fullness of God's best in my "now," there is none so great that will keep me from God's best in my "next."

My Promised Land—where milk and honey will be my portion and where God's perfection will be my end. That is what I am after. That is the day I am longing for, for me and for you. And until we make our final climb of surrender, may God grant us all the strength and wisdom to walk with sacred intention and with the promise of forever pulsing in our veins. Thus, I pray—

Give me the strength, Father, to walk this road in peace. Not to walk it with regrets, but rather with the firm faith that believes that the best is yet to be and that nothing from my past will keep me from knowing the full measure of your promise in my next. Thank you for the gift of my salvation that allows me the lavish expression of your eternal love and that fosters my vision toward unseen vistas and forever splendor. And until I get there, Father, protect my heart from the enemy's schemes that seek to steal, kill, and destroy my hope for a better tomorrow. Amen.

Peace in the desert

A further pause . . .

- What dreams of yesterday harbor regretful lament within your soul today?

- What consequences of your previous sin bear witness to the fact that there are some portions of the Promised Land that you may never know on this side of eternity?

- Please read Numbers 20:1-13 to discover the reasons behind Moses not being able to enter into the Promised Land. What was the reason? When has a similar response from your heart prevented you from knowing the fullness of God's promises?

- Deuteronomy 34 paints a beautiful portrait of Moses' death. What "gift" did God give to Moses in his final moments? Why is this significant?

a turn toward the better
(part two)

All these people were still living by faith when they died. They did not receive the things promised; they only saw them and welcomed them from a distance. And they admitted that they were aliens and strangers on the earth. People who say such things show that they are looking for a country of their own.
—Hebrews 11:13–14

Sometimes a moment comes to a soul and pulses so loudly within that if not spoken aloud, its voice buries long and deep, never to sing its intended melody. I learned a long time ago to tend to these moments. Part One of this devotional was one of those occasions, and without risking the integrity of the writing, I would like to unpack it a little more for you today.

Here is something you need to know: I don't climb Mt. Nebo in order to fast-forward into my "next." No, I climb Mt. Nebo so that I can better live in my "now." The view is breathtaking, even as it was for Moses. It reminds me that I am not home yet. It reminds me that for all of the promise that can be tasted on this side of eternity, there is a greater promise yet to come.

Moses was quickly ushered into his next without time enough to linger in his lust for the now. He moved from an earthly best into God's best in a single pause. This was a profound and sacred gift from God to this servant who lived the majority of his life as a desert dweller. For Moses, the Promised Land remained just out of reach. It simply was not his journey to make.

As it was with Moses, so it is with me. I am a desert dweller. It is not a popular vacation location in Christian circles. Most pulpits won't preach it, and most retreats won't teach it. Desert living simply doesn't package well with promotions aimed toward promise and abundance, lush and green.

I love the lush and green packages. I have purchased most of them, wanting more than anything to walk in them. But in my daily pilgrimage, I don't. Not usually. I've monitored the condition of my heart for years. I've tended to my spiritual pilgrimage and been careful to administer the daily checklists of a Christian obedience. I live Jesus each and every day, and I am bold enough—or perhaps just crazy enough—to admit that most of them walk dusty and hot and hard.

Now, before you send me your books on abundant living and on breaking free from my sands of struggle, you also need to know this: There is contentment to be found in the desert. I understand that this life is but a walk-through to a better country—a place of perfected promise, filled with God's abundance and plentiful reward. The incomparable glory that awaits

Peace in the desert

my arrival far outweighs the "all" of my now. Thus, my reasoning for my dusty roads and my willing acceptance of them.

Rather than trying to escape the desert and nearly wear myself out with the well-intentioned gymnastics of self-help and spiritual disciplines, I'm discovering an inner peace that comes to me because of my surrender to a desert's pause. It is a peace that roots back to the One who best understands the beauty of the desert journey.

Jesus Christ, the Son of the living God, knew what it was to walk a desert road. He lived it. His fleshly frame was cloaked with it. Like me, he was a pilgrim in search of a better country who managed to hold onto and cherish the sacred perspective of an unseen tomorrow. He never lost sight of it. He knew his Father was seeding in him an eternity that would drive away the sands of our temporal condition once and for all.

Calvary. Easter. Forever.

Jesus was and is the resurrection bloom that continues to bleed vibrant and alive, lush and green. Accordingly, strength and contentment for the dusty road I step are always available. Jesus steps the journey with me as I go.

I am a desert pilgrim. Perhaps you understand. Regardless of the reason for our detours in the desert, God asks us to trust him—to watch for him and to wait for the beauty of his unseen vistas and untouched blossoms. Even as he did for Moses, he will do for us.

Whether we are climbing the difficult mountains toward surrender or walking the glorious resurrection of such obedience, Jesus understands the gap between things visioned and things yet to be tasted. Either way, he is the bloom of both—in the desert and in promise. Thus, I pray—

For the mighty displays of your witness in all seasons of this journey, I thank you Lord. For your being the bloom along my weary and well-worn path, I bow in humble adoration. Thank you for your companioned beauty and your lasting aroma. I may never understand the fullness of my desert, but I will always endeavor to do so from your guiding watch within. Let me not balk at the summer's heat nor falter in my steps toward your forever. You are good and gracious to give me this day, regardless of how it unfolds. May I never discount the sacred value of the current road we travel together. Open my eyes to see, my mind to conceive, and my heart to believe that all is living as you intended for it to live—in me, through me, and most days, in spite of me . . . until my now crosses over into my next. Amen.

A further pause . . .

- Consider God's gift to Moses—the ushering of him into his eternal Promised Land with only a brief glimpse of the temporal Promised Land. In hindsight, do you think that Moses would have changed anything? How does this shape your vision for your current walk with God?

- Please read Hebrews 11:13–16. How do these verses parallel with the truth of an earthly desert pilgrimage?

- Describe an occasion when you've tasted a portion of God's Promised Land even in the midst of your heated desert obedience.

- What are some of the hopes that you carry in your heart for your tomorrow, both here on earth and in heaven?

the backside of forty

> *Remember how the LORD your God led you all the way in the desert these forty years, to humble you and to test you in order to know what was in your heart, whether or not you would keep his commands. . . . Observe the commands of the LORD your God, walking in his ways and revering him. For the LORD your God is bringing you into a good land.*
>
> —Deuteronomy 8:2, 6–7a

I like being in my forties. Forty years of living boast the wisdom of life experiences. At twenty, I would have preferred the wealth of wisdom of my now forty-three years, but life doesn't cadence in rhythm to a premature learning. Life unfolds to the melody of an eternal wisdom that exceeds my attempts at rushing the process.

Maturity of the heart and the mind takes time. It takes trials and joys. Tears and laughter. Getting it right and getting it wrong. Standing to show oneself approved and bowing in humility to garner that approval. It takes relationships. Lots of them. Family and friends and loves and community—all of whom weave their portion of influence into a wisdom that emerges because of a life lived and walked over a myriad of soils.

Maturity requires seasons and a willingness of heart and mind to be taught in all of them. Seasons that mirror:

- the color and change of fall's witness;
- the cold and empty of winter's embrace;
- the birth and blossom of spring's renewal;
- the hot and dry of summer's desert.

Forty years of living allow us the privilege of having walked them all. Some more than others. All seasons are parceled out for our growth—for our moving on to our perfection.

I haven't always believed this; many of my seasons were birthed because of sin—out of self-appointed choices or as a direct result of someone else's action. It is easy to rationalize their insignificance or deem them as spiritually meaningless, especially when they seem so far from a holy God's perfection and his ordaining of them therein.

Still and yet, he allows the seasons of our free will to be his shaping seasons. And while I think he might prefer that we learn some lessons in the classroom as opposed to in the wild and reckless ramblings of a field trip, God can and will work through our everything with his intended end in mind. No life experience is wasted in the economy of God's kingdom good.

This is very good news for a woman who has logged ample time in the hot and dry of a summer's desert. I don't fully understand why my life has been and is prone for a desert's embrace, but I do know that I walk in good company. God's Word is replete with people who, like me, wandered through their desert seasons and wondered about the sacred wisdom behind such a dusty pilgrimage.

The Israelites were one such people. They grappled with their desert in a way that most of us will never understand. Their desert cost them their lives. They didn't know the witness of a promised abundance because their sin exacted God's decision in the matter—death.

> But you—your bodies will fall in this desert. Your children will be shepherds here for forty years, suffering for your unfaithfulness, until the last of your bodies lies in the desert. For forty years—one year for each of the forty days you explored the land—you will suffer for your sins and know what it is like to have me against you.
> —Numbers 14:32–34

Our sin exacts the same if we are unwilling to yield to our Father's shaping and saving grace while in our desert times. Our desert dwelling requires a deeper level of faith—a perspective that exceeds the heat of a temporal difficulty because we understand that our God is bringing us into a good land, to a better soil that flows with the abundance and permanence of a sacred love, leveling our difficulty as a worthy struggle.

On the front end, we can't see it because we are prone to quick exits. In the desert, however, there are no doors marked accordingly—only miles and miles of unexpected sands that must be walked in order to enter into the spacious place that awaits us on the other side of a hard obedience. Unlike the Israelites, we are afforded grace. Despite our sins, we are offered the opportunity to continue in our desert pilgrimage with the promise of God's abundant "eternal" alongside.

They, however, stood on the edge of receiving God's promise, only to be turned back toward the Red Sea—pushed away from promise until forty years had exacted its sacred shaping upon their sons and daughters, readying them for its embrace (Numbers 14:25). It was:

- Forty years of a Father's humbling and testing.
- Forty years of trusting in a Father's provision for food and clothing.

- Forty years of laying oneself open for examination beneath the microscope of a Father's sacred purpose.
- Forty years of wondering about a Canaan that could be seen but that remained purposefully out of reach.
- Forty years of unknowns.
- Forty years of watching loved ones die.
- Forty years of regrets.
- Forty years of routine.
- Forty years of waiting.
- Forty years that belonged to God.
- Forty years that yielded an abundance as far as the eye could see and as deep as the heart could taste.

Indeed, I walk in good company. And while I think that after forty years of desert sands I would much prefer a different soil, I think that God prefers this one. Not because he relishes my struggle, but simply and profoundly because he relishes my relationship. In the desert, I am prone to seek him more. In the desert, I am forced to trust him more. In the desert, I am inclined toward bending more; because in the desert, my Father's "more" is more than enough to walk me home to my Canaan.

My Promised Land—my forever years that will breathe with the perfected wisdom of life experiences and with the eternal knowing that all of my seasons were allowed on purpose and for God's intended good. Thus, I pray—

Thank you for my seasons, Father, especially for the desert ones. Forgive me when I underestimate or dismiss their worth. Open up my heart and mind for the teaching and wisdom that comes with a desert journey. Let not my rush for the "exit" become my undoing. Instead, keep me there until I have gleaned and embedded the sacred learning that you have intended for me. Thank you for walking it with me. You are the privilege and penchant of my heart in all seasons. Amen.

A further pause . . .

- What season are you currently in—fall, winter, spring, summer? What makes it so?

- In what ways does the Christian journey mirror the Israelites' forty years of wandering in the desert?

- Is it easier or more difficult for you to seek and find God in your desert seasons? Why or why not?

- Take time to read Deuteronomy 8:1–9. Regardless of your age, list some of the ways that God has "kept" you during your life. How has his love for you proven faithful in all seasons?

4
Peace in the waters

He saw the disciples straining at the oars, because the wind was against them. About the fourth watch of the night he went out to them walking on the lake.

—Mark 6:48

from bitter to better

> *Then Moses led Israel from the Red Sea and they went into the Desert of Shur. For three days they traveled in the desert without finding water. When they came to Marah, they could not drink its water because it was bitter. (That is why the place is called Marah.) So the people grumbled against Moses, saying, "What are we to drink?"*
>
> —Exodus 15:22–24

Between the waters of a Red Sea's deliverance and the springs and palms of Elim, there almost always comes a Marah. A place of being stuck—moments of pause that force the question, "What are we to drink?"

I've been stuck recently.

The miraculous deliverance through the Red Sea is behind me, while the refreshment of Elim remains out of reach. Three days in the desert have temporarily suspended my earlier song:

> Sing to the Lord, for he is exalted. The horse and rider he has hurled into the sea.
>
> —Exodus 15:21

That kind of deliverance always births a melody. But when the heat comes—the walk of faith amidst the sweltering temperatures of an unseen tomorrow—the melody of faith often diminishes to a faint whisper. My focus on my next drink buries the recent memory of a walled sea that was stacked on my behalf by a God who has promised to walk me safely home.

I forget to remember him, and all too quickly, I come to my Marah in the matter. Bitter waters. Waters that were never meant to quench a thirst, yet the only well within the visible surroundings. Waters that, when tasted, remind me of my inescapable need for a drink.

Water. Sometimes a friend. Sometimes a traitor. Always our necessity. We cannot escape our need for its refreshment. There are times when we are inundated with its abundance and times when we are parched by its absence. But between those seasons, when the balance pours predictably, water receives little, if any, of our thoughtful consideration.

Water is our neglected assumption until water roars its voice in autonomous opposition, thus forcing our notice. Whether through droughts, floods, storms, hurricanes, or seasons of famine, water plays a vital role in our survival. We can't live without it, but living with it sometimes requires a delicate balance.

Peace in the waters

The Israelites struggled to find that balance. Behind them? A faith walk that had conquered a sea's impossibility. Ahead of them? A faith walk that required a trust in a "yet-to-be-visioned-and-tasted" Promised Land. It didn't take long for them to find their complaint. Our grumbling walks in similar stride.

When faith walks thirstily, faith talks loudly. Sometimes through to deliverance, sometimes through to bitterness—to moments of longing for the cool waters of yesterday's captivity rather than the seemingly undrinkable wet of today's freedom.

It is a short leap from faith to flesh. But from *flesh* to *faith*? A long climb and a stretched-out obedience that requires a trust in an unseen future with an unseen God. And that which cannot be seen is often traded in for that which can be touched and tasted and taken to temporarily satisfy thirst, even when it swallows bitterly.

So how do we walk it? How are we to navigate our thirst between a sea's deliverance and the abundance of Elim? What do we do when we find ourselves stuck at Marah, knowing that our Father never intended for us to drink "bitter," but means for us to drink better—holier and purer and full, with a cup that never runs empty?

We do what Moses did. We allow God his cross in the matter. We cast his wood into the bitterness and allow the redemption of Calvary's gift to sweeten the wetness with a quenching that keeps . . . that lasts . . . that endures and that fills us with enough faith to walk us on to Elim.

When we find ourselves stuck at Marah, we have a choice to make. We can wander around with a thirsty cup of "bitter" in our hands, or we can drink from a better cup that ladles from an intentional pause at the foot of the cross. Either way, a cup is required, because water is our necessity. One cup leaves us where we are—stuck and immovable and content to wander in soured surroundings. The other leads us through the desert—full and fresh and filled with a faith that welcomes the sweetened release of a wood's working.

Marah is not without answers. Stuck doesn't have to stay wedged within the sands of an aimless desperation. God is still in the business of providing his cup to his children. In plenty and in want, the living water of Jesus Christ is the holy cup that will fill us fully as we navigate the sands of deliverance between a Red Sea and a Promised Land that is closer now than it has ever been.

If today you have arrived at Marah, confused and concerned about your need for a drink, don't allow your "bitter" to be your portion. Instead, find your pause, open up God's Word, and allow the cleansing work of grace to sweeten your moments of thirst. Being stuck at Marah can lead to your eventual bitterness. But being stuck at Marah *with God* will always lead to something better—something lasting that fuels our faith for the walk home to our Father's forever.

That is his promise to each one of us today. Thus, I pray—

Father, I thank you for your Word that promises its effectual power in my life, even when I am blinded to its workings. I thank you for my Marah moments that force me to pause and to contemplate my next drink. Allow my thirst to be my entrance into your redeeming presence that fills my cup with enough faith to walk it through. For my Red Sea deliverance, I thank you. For the abundance of Elim, I bless you. And for the pilgrimage in between, I rest in you, knowing that your cup of better awaits my surrender. Thank you for the cross that allows me your living water in all seasons of this journey. Amen.

A further pause . . .

- Consider your life. When have you tasted a Red Sea's deliverance, the bitter waters of Marah, the abundant waters of Elim?

- Where are you currently in your journey? Can you trace God's hand in your steps?

- Compare Exodus 15:22–27 with John 4:10–14 and Hebrews 12:2. What connection exists between the wood's "necessary" and the water's "sweet"?

- Prayerfully consider any areas in your life where your Marah remains. Humbly confess your bitterness before God, and allow his sweet grace to fall over what remains.

the beauty of a backward glance

Be still, and know that I am God.

—Psalm 46:10a

Shaping seasons. We've all had them. Times in our lives chronicled by life-changing situations that force the issue of faith. Perhaps you're living in one right now. If so, you walk it without the benefit of hindsight. You walk it forward, hoping for an eventual backward glance. I understand. I've walked this road on multiple occasions.

But today I have the privilege of a backward glance to one of those shaping seasons that occurred ten years ago. It's not a cherished memory, for that season was hard fought, hard lived, and barely endured. I don't imagine I will ever again experience the spectrum of emotions that I felt during that time. My heart might not survive the process. Even this morning, as I perused the vast storehouse of my written thoughts during 1999, tears welled from the prick of its thorny reminder.

Still and yet, there is worth in the remembering because of the eternal shaping wrought forth in me through the suffering. It was a suffering season that changed me. A sacred season named Hurricane Floyd.

Unless you've personally walked through the valley of a hurricane's devastation, you cannot fully appreciate the depth of its embrace. You can witness it via the television screen, still photography, the Internet, and the newspaper, but unless you're living it in real color, your knowledge is skewed.

Not that I would wish your literal participation. Some storms are better viewed from a distance. Some lessons are better learned secondhand. But there are some storms allowed their fury within our lives, because storms, perhaps more than any other mode of divine forging, hold the immediate and forceful capacity to:

- shake our complacency;
- shatter our comfort;
- shift our concerns;
- shape our character.

Peace in the waters

Storms are slaps in the face—wake-up calls to take notice and to get busy. This would be my portion in 1999. Even after a decade of separation from that season, my recall of those moments is vivid and poignant and worthy of some words this day.

There are so many things I could tell you. So many things I recall. So many lessons learned because of Floyd. But for all the stresses and strains, fears and failings that undoubtedly forged a teaching within my soul, there is one lesson—one thread of purpose—that weaves lasting and true . . .

People. Victims and volunteers alike.

During that time, I partook of the purest portion of human expression. Love was our measure, poured forth into the hearts of individuals who needed its embrace more than food or clothing or a home to call their own. Love walked as God intended.

We moved from that town a year later. I won't lie; it was a welcome relief for our family and the necessary step to save a marriage and a ministry. But we didn't leave without some love in our hearts. Recently, that sacred thread of love fueled my husband's return to the place of our Floyd's fury to bury one of God's saints.

Mrs. Edna was a precious woman who gave us her love when others wouldn't. A woman who saw past the color of our skin and into the pulse of our hearts. A woman who laughed and lived, despite the carnage going on around her. A woman who kept the fires of her hearth burning, even when Floyd's waters desired to extinguish the flames. A woman who taught me the sacred value of a storm—not so much through her words, but through her actions that spoke a teaching far greater than man's chronicling of the event.

She gave me her friendship, and in doing so, allowed me some sacred purpose in a season that rarely made sense. She, and others like her, painted the beauty in my backward glance. And while I don't frequent Floyd's memories in my mind very often, when I do, I do so with some joy and some thankfulness. Not for the menacing devastation of floodwaters, but for the relationships that were birthed through their cleansing.

Maybe an unnamed storm lurks in and around your life this day. It has slapped you in the face with a wake-up call that forces your notice and that asks you to get busy. Just exactly how that "busy" will breathe, I'm not sure. But of this I am certain: When storms slap, storms require. When storms subside, memories remain. And therein lies the connection. What remains threads back to what is required. Memories paint purposefully if the steps taken to paint them are walked confidently and with the trust that God is after a masterpiece in the end. Otherwise, they simply paint bitterly.

I couldn't see God's masterpiece in September of 1999. But today my remembrances emerge into a clearer vision. Especially the memory of a woman who walked that season better than I and who lived her life better than most. She is the beauty of my backward glance. Her friendship to me and my family weaves a portion of purpose into that very difficult season of requirement.

I pray that you, too, have the benefit of a beautiful look back on your trying seasons. If not now, then soon. Shaping and beauty walk their own timetable, and when visioned through the lenses of a Father's best intentions, they walk thankful for the privilege of participation . . . .

Even in a hurricane. Thus, I pray—

Father, paint our lives with intention this day. May the beauty of heaven's purpose be allowed in our vision. Where we lack strength, bolster our hearts and our frames for the walk. Where we lack wisdom, give us insight into the depths of your understanding. Where we lack patience, give us feet for the long haul. And where we lack love, pour the truth of Calvary's love into us through the power of your Spirit so that we may share it with others. I thank you for the hurricane that rudely and appropriately interrupted my life and forced me to my knees. Weave its beauty into my masterpiece for always. Amen.

A further pause . . .

- When have you personally experienced great tragedy in your life?

- Describe some of the most valuable relationships you encountered during that season. What made them so?

- Storms have a way of bringing out the best and the worst in humanity. When have you known this to be true?

- Consider the raising of Lazarus as found in John 11:1–44. Take time to read the words of Jesus—the red-lettered words—in isolation. Read them a second time, out loud, if you can. Now, imagine Jesus speaking these words over your season of tragedy. Jesus' intervention in your life, both then and now, is the beauty in your backward glance. Can you trace his love for you, even when it was difficult to see through the pain?

a sacred reduction

> *Then Noah built an altar to the LORD and, taking some of all the clean animals and clean birds, he sacrificed burnt offerings on it. The LORD smelled the pleasing aroma and said in his heart: "Never again will I curse the ground because of man, even though every inclination of his heart is evil from childhood. And never again will I destroy all living creatures, as I have done."*
>
> —Genesis 8:20–21

Floods reduce.

Whether in the tangible, or in the unseen, less measurable ways, floods reduce. They purge and purify. They eliminate with precision and intention. They forcefully suggest that some things—some lives—are worthy of reduction.

This seems an odd fit alongside the covenantal promises of Genesis 8 and 9, yet our Father allows the flood its cleansing in our lives. Sometimes in the literal. Sometimes more veiled. But all times for a reason. While navigating its tempestuous cleansing, we are rarely given the privilege of foresight—those beginning understandings about the sacred worth of our reduction.

But when hindsight reaches its climax, when the storms have passed and the waters have receded, there are those rare few who have willingly embraced their reduction. Not with anger and with bitterness, but rather with a heart that is courageously thankful for the gift of another day. For the beauty of a sun's rise. For the grace that affords them a walk upon the freshly-baptized soil of a difficult reduction.

Miss Mable was one such soul who wisely reasoned the depth of her flood's embrace. Her flood? Hurricane Floyd. Her response? To build an altar of gratitude within her heart rather than with the few earthly treasures that remained. Floyd reduced her tangibles in swift measure but was unable to reduce her faith in the one God who had allowed her another day's breath in addition to her previous ninety-two years.

Other than her fragile frame, little else remained for Miss Mable when she arrived at our relief center on that crisp October morning. Our church's fellowship hall became a makeshift store for those who had known the reduction of Floyd's waters. I was in charge of organizing the generous donations of items and their distribution—an overwhelming task, matched only by the overwhelming need that presented itself within our little community.

When I saw Miss Mable, I knew that I needed to be the one to walk her through the process. Her ancient beauty and the confusion that outlined her graceful frame drew me to her. This would be a difficult journey for her. Thus, together we made the rounds through the various tables of canned goods, cleaning supplies, hygiene products, blankets, towels, and the like.

It all seemed too overwhelming for Mable. She simply stared at me and uttered the uncertainty of her heart: "I know there are things that I need. I simply can't make my mind think in such ways." I understood. I had been living those days of reduction alongside her. Floyd's aftermath could not be calmed by a single visit to our relief center.

Feeling her frustration, I continued to pack her box without asking any questions. As we made our way to the door, Miss Mable spied a collection of new, large-print Bibles that were stacked near the exit. Her demeanor quickly changed, and she humbly asked me if they were "for the taking."

I assured her that they needed a good home. Mable explained to me that her treasured family Bible had been claimed by the waters of Floyd. She also told me that this was the one thing that she could get her mind around.

Mable found her letter from God that day—the Word of God. Timeless and true no matter the wrapping. No matter the date of publication. No matter the version or translation. Mable rediscovered her foundation in that moment. She found her incentive for moving beyond her pain.

That day, she built an altar of worship, and never has an aroma been more pleasing to our God. He smelled her sacrifice from afar, and he sent forth his Word to heal her and to embolden her spirit for the journey ahead. Floyd's reduction may have stripped away her earthly treasures, but in doing so, it highlighted and gave stage to the one treasure that endures. The one truth that, once tasted, remains as the benchmark for all further and eternal sustenance:

God's Word.

It's been over a decade since that season of difficult decrease. Mable has since moved from her faith in an unseen God to the seen and tangible reward of his literal embrace. And while I don't revisit Floyd very often in my mind, when I do, I am drawn to the remembrance of this woman who better understood the sacred value of a flood's reduction. She was not embittered by the water's embrace; instead, she was enlivened by its pulse and thankful for another day to breathe its witness.

Indeed, floods reduce. They disrobe and diminish our externals so that the internal life is exposed. If there is no lasting word to sustain us, the only altars built will be the ones memorialized with the words of self-reliance and anointed with the oil of independent unction. That kind of reduction will never seed purpose. Instead it will continue to script diminishment and dissolve into hearts that were never meant to go it alone but, instead, were seeded with eternity in mind.

However, if the living Word is present, is alive and active in the internal soil of a soul when the floodwaters shout their reduction, the altar that remains is an everlasting strength—an exposed and sacred memorial that breathes the true witness of eternal increase and a lasting Word. And that kind of consecrated reduction, my friends, is worth the aroma of surrender.

More of God. Less of me. Thus, I pray—

Reduce me, Lord, as needed. Send your waters to cleanse my life from the external trappings of a cluttered faith. Strip away my many things so that the one thing—the one You—receives the glorious exposure of a flood's reduction. Let my faith prove genuine, even when the surrender walks hard and seemingly void of purpose. Let my sacrifice be pleasing in your heart, Lord, and send forth your Word to heal me and to enliven me for the gift of a new beginning. Amen.

Peace in the waters

A further pause . . .

- Describe a time in your life when you've known the "reduction" of flood waters—either in the literal or spiritual sense.

- What was your most difficult "surrender" in that time of reduction? What made it so?

- Miss Mable lost her treasured family Bible; her joy returned with the discovery of its replacement. How do you feel about the treasure of God's Word? Is your Bible well-worn or simply well-preserved?

- Take a moment to read a portion of Moses' final words to the Israelites before his death in Deuteronomy 32:44–47. How do Moses' instructions reflect the treasure that Miss Mable rediscovered in our relief center?

the glorious renaissance of a flooded fury

> *And when Jesus had cried out again in a loud voice, he gave up his spirit. At that moment the curtain of the temple was torn in two from top to bottom. The earth shook and the rocks split. . . . When the centurion and those with him who were guarding Jesus saw the earthquake and all that had happened, they were terrified, and exclaimed, "Surely he was the Son of God!"*
> —Matthew 27:50–51, 54

It's not an easy walk from darkness to light, from surrender to victory, from death to life. However, it is ours to pilgrim if we are to truly wear the cloaking of a resurrected life. Somewhere between our stripping down to nothing and our dressing up with God's everything comes a journey that requires a faith willing to contend with the elements that seed us, shape us, and grow us into fruitful harvest. It is a journey often fraught with a:

- storm rather than the serene;
- valley rather than a mountaintop;
- desert rather than the green and lush of abundance;
- flood, rather than the dry of a routine usual.

Such would be the shaping season in my life nearly a decade ago. Hurricane Floyd swept through the doors of our little community with a relentless fury that not only flooded us in the physical but also that deluged our emotional and spiritual reserves with an unyielding pulse that forced the issue of our faith.

It stripped me bare. Day after day, week after week, until seven months had passed, and I could barely find enough strength to continue. Shaping seasons are like that. They strip and reduce with very little fruit-bearing along the way. When the cost seems too great—when the output exceeds the input—the void left behind screams its emptiness through all manner of voices.

Mine screamed lonely. Silently. Withdrawn and without the understanding of another alongside to share my struggle. And even though the waters of Floyd had dried up some months earlier, I continued to drown in the aftermath of its overflow. This walk of obedience may have been my "necessary," but at the time, it proffered more like my ruin. And when I reached my end, when I readied my heart for a departure to anywhere but there, God sent me a rope.

He gave me a vine. Literally.

Peace in the waters

I found it in a house scheduled for demolition. In addition to its four feet of wet, termites had exacted their toll on this 100-year-old structure. The house stood at a tilt, and little effort would be required to send it to its grave. Prior to its demise, I wanted to document this portion of Floyd's history with my camera.

I took a final survey of the structure by walking its circumference. It was then that I saw them. The last and final living remnants from 104 Lower Street. Vines, clinging beautifully to the white brick chimney on the right side of the house and reaching almost to its top. I snapped a photograph, and moments later, the house surrendered to the blows of the hammer.

It didn't take long. I watched it wobble a time or two, but on the third blow, the house collapsed. What once stood as a witness to a century of family living, now lay on the ground in piles of splintered boards and dust. That chimney and those vines? Well, they took a bit longer. They were the last to fall.

It was as if those vines provided the chimney a stronger protection than the rest of the house. As the blows crashed upon that final chord of life, I strained to see the green rope as it fell to the ground. Indeed, it fell, and before the work crew hauled the remains off to the local dump, I quickly made my way over to them to survey their surrender.

Tears came, and through my blurred vision I spotted a most unusual gift. Green. Unbroken. Dusty. Yet somehow, still reaching its witness far above the pile that symbolized this final ending. Life, reaching forth and calling for notice. A garden of mercy amidst a pile of surrender. A hope springing to life in the middle of a final crucifixion.

Vines, strong and secure, journeying alongside until the very end. Weeping their protective tears with each blow of the hammer. Moving into a new place of surrender. Buried in a tomb of mortar and wood, yet springing forth just enough for me to catch the moment—a necessary moment so that I could receive a gift from God on a day when I needed the truth of their witness.

Sometimes it takes a demolition to see the green. Sometimes our brokenness brings such a death that all that remains is the Vine, reminding us that life issues forth from the surrender, that the taking of the home—the heart—becomes the sacrificial necessity for the birth of a glorious renaissance.

Christ understands the walk of a sacrificial requirement. He lived the surrender and the death of a hammered obedience so that his light and his life could be ours for always. He was willing to contend with the elements of his sacred shaping so that we could know ours. And when the final blow sent him to his tomb, the earth shook and the rocks split; and for those who stood by to witness his fall, God gave them the truth of a Vine's witness:

"Surely he was the Son of God" (Mark 15:39). Surely, he still *is*.

May you, throughout your journey to the cross, sense the guarded protection of God's clinging Vine. May you walk with Christ into the garden of surrender, remembering all the while that true light, vibrant living, and sure victory will be the punctuation that springs forth from your necessary ashes.

Life in the Vine. My peaceful rest. Thus, I pray—

In the name of the Father, and of the Son, and of the abiding Holy Spirit, Amen.

A further pause . . .

- When have you conceded your "life" to the process of demolition so that restoration could begin?

- Read John 15:1–8. Describe the importance of the Vine as the thread that connects the old with the new.

- Describe the moment/process of your own glorious renaissance. What life experiences preceded that awakening? What are some of the most valuable treasures birthed because of it?

- Are there any areas of your life that need the benefit of the hammer this day? If so, surrender them to God, knowing that your Father is after a masterpiece and is faithful to complete your journey with his good and perfected end.

a sea's deliverance

That day, when evening came, he said to his disciples, "Let us go over to the other side." Leaving the crowd behind, they took him along, just as he was, in the boat. There were also other boats with him. A furious squall came up, and the waves broke over the boat, so that it was nearly swamped. . . . He got up, rebuked the wind and said to the waves, "Quiet! Be still!" Then the wind died down and it was completely calm.

—Mark 4:35–37, 39

There is no sea so tempestuous that it would prevent my Father's crossing it on my behalf. There is no sea too daunting for his journey of grace. The waves that threaten to submerge me are but the bridge that he uses to walk his steps of rescue. Steps that sometimes require the breadth of a sea's separation. Steps that always require a love that exceeds my understanding and that forgives my self-centered attempts at release. Steps that issue from the heart of a Father who says, "Let us go over to the other side."

The theology of "the other side." It was there at the beginning, when humanity first chose to distance itself from Eden's grip of grace. Man and woman took to their boat and paddled the waters of a willful disobedience, until they landed on the shores of a prisoned isolation—the other side. Alone. Naked. Scarred by the chains of sin's grip and entombed within sin's perimeter. A desperate location. A fatal resignation to all things temporal and fleeting.

Indeed, it was a difficult reach to that "other side," one that would require the outstretched arms of a God who understood the breadth of sin's chasm. One who knew just how long and wide and high and deep his love would have to extend in order to arrive at the shores of our chosen disobedience—the other side of an amazing grace.

God has always been about our other side. While always operating on behalf of the hundred percent, our Father lovingly tends to the one percent—you and me. The cry of the individual, amidst the shouts of the many, never goes unnoticed. Instead, God dispatches his grace to tend to our pleas and to free us from our chains, especially when our chains have driven us to solitary places that chant their tombed dissonance amongst the squeals and squalor of a pig's refrain.

Gerasa—the other side. A region boasting the presence of Gentiles, hosting the herds of a ceremonially unclean livestock, and confining the demons of one man in need of release. Definitely not a favorite locale for a righteous Hebrew, yet exactly the intended destination for the most righteous of them all.

Peace in the waters

Jesus could have stayed where he was—on the banks of man's applause, teaching his truth through parables to a crowd who welcomed his voice. Instead, he chose to bring his truth to the one voice whose disdain was evident from the beginning and whose welcome would signal a showdown between heaven's grace and hell's confinement: "What do you want with me, Jesus, Son of the Most High God? Swear to God that you won't torture me!" (Mark 5:7).

Jesus chose the journey to the other side of hell because on that "other side" stood one man in need of his answer and in danger of making hell his permanent forever. Jesus didn't come to torture the one. He came to release the one from the torment of the many.

The theology of the other side.

The boat ride that began with the soothing rock of the Galilean waters became a treacherous journey through a fierce storm. There is a connection between the two—between the calm of heaven and the disdain of hell. Whenever the freedom of a soul hangs in the balance, there is always a sacred tension that requires a response. We may not see it, but even when our eyes are blinded to the strain between the two, nature bears witness to the conflict; in this case it was in a furious squall.

Whether we are in the boat with Jesus on our way to minister on the other side, on the shore awaiting the gift of God's grace or walking on the waters with a faith that bobbles in rhythm to the pulse of the sea, when storms come, they bring their questions with them. If we aren't anchored to the correct theology, we are prone to jumping ship, hiding in tombs, and sinking beneath the waves of a storm that was never meant to be our undoing but rather to be our strengthened understanding.

Jesus journeyed with his theology in tow. He was not surprised by the sea's embrace. He wasn't vulnerable to the sound of its voice. Rather, he simply and profoundly embraced it with his owns words of ownership: "Quiet, be still!"

In that moment, a sea found its silence so that a Savior could find the other side—the one percent of humanity worth the fury and the fuss of hell's wrath as displayed and, ultimately, dispelled within the waters of a necessary obedience. Jesus arrived on the shores of his intention, and with the same breath that calmed the waters, he breathed release over a soul whose torture took up final residency within two thousand irritated and confused pigs on their way to a watery grave.

The one left behind? Finally free, on his knees, and "dressed and in his right mind."

I, too, have stood on the shores of Gerasa, bound by sin and chains that longed to keep me in my tombed existence. From a distance, the God of the hundred percent saw my need and forged the storms of Calvary's cross to become the God of the one percent. He called me by name, put me in my right mind, and covered my nakedness with his robes of righteousness. His words of release are now the unchained Word in my heart and my required witness to a world that needs to embrace the theology of "the other side."

Perhaps this day your heart longs for his ship to pull into harbor and for his feet to walk upon the soil of your life and call it holy, call it his. For every chain that Satan would seek to wrap around your soul, there is a Word from God that will unlock your captivity and set your spirit free. If Gerasa is your portion, then Christ is your answer. He has come to the other side on your behalf. Not because he has to, but rather because his love for the one—for you—compels him to do so.

Bow the knee and humble the heart. Your Savior's ship has landed. Thus, I pray—

Thank you, Father, for the stormy seas that have brought you to the shores of my rescue. Thank you for the love that fueled your journey and kept you focused on the needs of the one, despite the cries of the many. I am humbled by your willingness to come to me in my confinement and speak freedom over my chains. You have clothed me with your grace and renewed my mind in a right and holy direction. Let the witness of your lavish expression on my behalf be the fuel that carries me to "the other side" so that others might share in this freedom. Amen.

A further pause . . .

- Take a few minutes to consider this entire teaching from Jesus as found in Mark 4:35–5:20. How are the two stories connected?

- When have you known a similar captivity in your own Gerasa? What chains kept you there? Describe the process of grace that released you from your confinement.

- Please read the parable of the "lost sheep" in Matthew 18:10–14. How does the story mirror the theology of "the other side"?

- How might God be asking you to journey the sea on behalf of another?

5
Peace in the suffering

When Jesus saw her weeping, and the Jews who had come along with her also weeping, he was deeply moved in spirit and troubled. "Where have you laid him?" he asked. "Come and see, Lord," they replied. Jesus wept.

—John 11:33–35

unseen glances

Therefore we do not lose heart. Though outwardly we are wasting away, yet inwardly we are being renewed day by day. For our light and momentary troubles are achieving for us an eternal glory that far outweighs them all. So we fix our eyes not on what is seen, but on what is unseen. For what is seen is temporary, but what is unseen is eternal.

—2 Corinthians 4:16–18

She captures my thoughts today. How could she not?

A tragic ending to a fragile young life has made the national headlines, stunning the Christian community and forcing a family to deal with the unexpected and unwelcomed intruder named "death."

The five-year-old daughter of a well-known singer and songwriter has left the arms of her earthly parents to make her entrance into the arms of her heavenly Father. A life gone too soon. Five years of loving a child is simply not enough. It is a grief that struggles to reconcile fact with faith. A hard reckoning in my opinion, but one that becomes necessary for all who experience its candid and cold embrace.

My mind and heart cannot frame it. It strikes a chord within me. Death does that. It strikes. It resounds. It penetrates the silence with the deafening chorus of a truth better left unsung, or so we think. It is a truth that follows our entrance into this world. A truth that will mark our exit from it. A truth that simply and poetically scripts . . .

We were born to die.

From the moment we first breathed the air of our temporal existence, we began our journey toward our eternal home. It is the way of things. It always has been. We shouldn't be surprised by death's arrival; still and yet, it almost always cuts with a precision that leaves us to grapple with its certainty.

And unless the Lord returns in our lifetime, death will be our required portion.

The apostle Paul asks us to keep our focus in times of trouble. To understand that our temporary afflictions are achieving, accomplishing, and producing an eternal glory for us that far exceeds our pain. To perceive the unseen and to believe that the unseen surpasses our current fracture. To keep heart, even though our hearts shatter and scatter with the winds of adversity that howl loudly and break hard.

Good truth, but a difficult striving; in our flesh, death always limits perspective. Our flesh cries out for the temporary, for the immediate, for the right now. A tomorrow's work will have to wait, because today's tears are all that can be absorbed.

How can anyone begin to walk in an understanding that limits the "current" to seemingly nothing more than a monument to learning, becoming, and moving on to a yet-to-be-grasped perfection? How can death be parametered into a pill that swallows smoothly? What do we do with a grief whose bite seems lethal and whose gnaw continually chews? How do we fix our eyes on anything but the casket that currently cradles our sorrow?

How indeed?

Paul doesn't ask us to turn away from a casket's view. He doesn't ask us to get over our grief quickly and move beyond. Instead, he encourages us to gaze more deeply into death's frame. His thoughts are not callous or removed—a script meant for a stage some two thousand years ago. No, Paul's words are exactly the words of comfort we need in times of sorrow, because a human life is more than flesh and blood. Our fragile frames embody both the seen and the unseen—the temporal and the eternal.

God has created us in his image (Genesis 1:26–27) and placed eternity into the hearts of all people (Ecclesiastes 3:11). This sets us apart from all of his other created works. Thus, when Paul asks us to fix our eyes on the unseen and the eternal in times of momentary affliction, he gives us permission to mourn our loss. Our Creator allows us the same, for with our tears, we acknowledge a human life for what it is: A created flesh covering an eternal pulse. The seen cloaking the unseen. The momentary shrouding the never-ending.

This is why our grief is real. This is why we can say goodbye to "things" with little fret, but when it comes to people, our fret is palpable and deep. This is why we can find hope, even in the midst of a tremendous grief. For when death visits a life, perfection finds its home. The unseen begins when the seen embraces its end. The eternal breathes its fullest when the momentary breathes its last. The glory finds its brilliance when the temporary finds its dullness. The heavens chorus their applause when the earth silences its song.

And while it's true that "we were born to die," the greater and final truth is this: We die so that we can fully live—eternally. Without restraints. Without affliction. Without sorrow. Without endings. Without goodbyes.

This is the perspective I need today as I live and breathe the truth of a family's grief. A young child has found her life, even as her fragile frame has found its death. It is the same for each one of us as we draw ever nearer to tasting a similar portion.

Peace for the Journey

Let us not shrink back from dealing with our grief. Let us not hide from its bitter taste. Instead, let us bravely acknowledge the hope that pulses beyond every death. Let us fix our eyes on the Creator, who fashioned each person to breathe an earthly life's span and then to breathe an eternal life. He is where I'm headed, friends. And should we never meet face-to-face on this side of forever, I will meet you there, where we will share in our Father's happiness for always. Thus, I pray—

Keep us to the road of our forever, Father. Let us not shrink back in our pilgrimage towards you, but rather strengthen our resolve for what lies ahead. May the unseen of your marvelous forever be the hope that carries us onward and upward until the unexplainable is made sight and we grasp the full intention behind death's pause. You are the treasure I long to behold. Until then, may your Spirit continue his work in me, reminding me of the treasure I now embrace. You are enough, Father— yesterday, today, and forever. Amen.

Peace in the suffering

A further pause . . .

- Describe a time when you experienced a death that seemed unexplainable and unnecessary. What made it the most difficult? How did you resolve your feelings in the matter?

- According to 1 Thessalonians 4:13–18, how are we able to grieve the loss of a loved one with hope?

- What are some "seen" things in your life right now that make it difficult to focus on the unseen treasures of God?

- What particular "unseen" do you most long for and why?

- Write out 2 Corinthians 4:16–18 on an index card and meditate on the depth of its truth. Remember it the next time your "seen" threatens the hope of your "unseen."

a cup that would not pass

Going a little farther, he fell with his face to the ground and prayed, "My Father, if it is possible, may this cup be taken from me. Yet not as I will, but as you will."

—Matthew 26:39

We all have them.

Allowed cups—portions of drink that become ours to swallow.

Some swallow sweetly. Some linger with their bitterness. Some make sense, and some extend beyond reason. Regardless of their taste, they are our consumption. God has allowed them to touch our lips, the effects sometimes lingering long and hard upon the palate of our will.

Jesus drank from one such cup.

Cup. "Porterion" in the Greek. A word in Matthew's gospel that roots back to the metaphorical Hebrew language, meaning, "lot, portion, under the emblem of a cup which God presents to be drunk, either for good or for evil. In the NT the cup of sorrow, meaning the bitter lot which awaited the Lord in His sufferings and death."[6]

Long before Christ knew the confines of his cross, he made a decision to embrace the cup of the cross. It was the deepest drink of suffering ever portioned out to humanity. His Father assigned it to him before the foundation of the world. This cup would not go down easily, but it would go down. Deep down. All the way down from his head to his feet, until love's redeeming work was done.

God's will in the matter trumped his Son's plea to the contrary. In the end, Jesus' decision to drink the cup was based upon his knowledge of what stood to be lost by his rejection of it: *us*.

We stood on the other side of his hard surrender. We were the purpose behind his unparalleled obedience to partake of the cup that carried our salvation. It was the cup that would pass from our lips onto his because our lips are not capable of such sacrifice. Our blood bleeds temporal. Christ's blood sheds eternal.

No wonder Jesus' stern rebuke of Peter's misguided devotion and unbridled emotion as recorded in John 18:11:

Put your sword away! Shall I not drink from the cup the Father has given me?

Peace in the suffering

Jesus understood that to forsake this cup would be to forsake his Father's perfect plan for creation. Some would argue that he didn't have a choice in the matter; I would simply offer up his sorrowful pleas as proof that the human flesh always has a choice in the matter. Jesus' choice was rooted in the surrendering of his flesh to a greater purpose—that of living out his Father's intentions. Our choices are almost always rooted otherwise—toward our intentions and what we deem best in the immediate.

Suffering in the flesh is a difficult connection to abide. Our wills aren't wired for the pain. Our wills are wired for the "easy," for portioned cups that swallow painlessly; thus, the rub when the cup of another flavor finds our lips. We are tempted to refuse its swallow because we refuse to believe that the uncomfortable—the painful and difficult—is often the cup that will most perfectly lead us toward our becoming mature in the faith.

Why suffering? Why hard? Why not something more palatable rather than more contrary?

Because there is a dividing line between the life we now live in the flesh and the life we long to live in faith. To get from a posture of "my will be done" to "Thy will be done" requires a greater work in our hearts. Standing between the two is a difficult "letting go" of the one so as to embrace the other. Sometimes it's an easy leap. Sometimes we get a pass. But when we don't, when suffering offers up her cup to us and a harder swallow becomes our requirement, how do we respond?

Left to ourselves, we will never willingly imbibe. Our cups of suffering may go down, but without the tender guidance and understanding of God's Spirit within, they often swallow hard, leaving a bitter aftertaste. God understands the requirement. He knows what he is asking of us because he asked it of his own Son. And because of Jesus' willing "yes" in the matter, we are better enabled to offer ours.

It doesn't mean that we desire it or welcome the pain because of it. It simply and profoundly means that we accept our suffering cups because we understand a greater gain awaits us on the other side of our surrender. And that gain, my friends, cannot be measured according to our pain. There is nothing we will suffer on this side of eternity that will exceed the worth and glory of heaven. *Nothing*.

To think otherwise, to believe that somehow our current suffering will exchange in equal measure for a soon-to-be glory, is to minimize a grace that cannot be purchased. God's love cannot be appraised and quantified according to our suffering. We don't get more because we suffer more. We simply get more because our God *is* more. More than enough. More than willing. More than able. More than wonderful. More than anticipation. More than expectation. More than anything and everything we could ever imagine. God's more exceeds our momentary less.

Thus, whatever cups are allowed us in this current season of living, whether easy or whether hard, you and I have been given God's strength for the swallowing. They may not make sense in the "here and now," but when we get home to God's "there and then," all will make perfect sense. Truth will be revealed in a final glory that will validate our current sufferings as purposeful and needful.

To explain it beyond this would be to limit the mystery that belongs to God alone. We don't have to understand it on the front side of eternity. We simply must believe that perfect wisdom exists and, therefore, concede our cups to our Father, who will pour out understanding in due time and in full measure.

It won't be long in coming; but until then, we must embrace the cup allowed our lips. It is our privilege to do so because it was to our Father's glory that our Savior did so. Thus, I pray—

Press our lips to our necessary and allowed cups, Father. Keep us drinking in full anticipation of an understanding that is soon to be ours. Thank you for your willing drink of surrender, which allows us full access to heaven's glory. Humbly, we receive the gift. May the pouring out of your grace bring about the willing pouring out of our hearts. You are our portioned cup, Lord. Pour yourself through me this day. Amen.

Peace in the suffering

A further pause . . .

- What cups have been allowed your lips in recent days? The cup of _____. Please list.

- How are you drinking from those cups—with willingness or with rebellion?

- What do the following scriptures teach us about "suffering"?

    Romans 8:15–17

    2 Corinthians 1:3–7

    2 Corinthians 4:16–18

    1 Peter 4:12–13

- Read the full account of Jesus' suffering prior to the cross as found in Matthew 26:36–56. Record Jesus' responses to his suffering cup in verses 38, 39, 42, 46, 50, 54, and 56. How does his willing "yes" embolden you for yours?

a sacred covering

Do your best to come to me quickly, for Demas, because he loved this world, has deserted me and has gone to Thessalonica. . . . Only Luke is with me. Get Mark and bring him with you, because he is helpful to me in my ministry. . . . When you come, bring the cloak that I left with Carpus at Troas, and my scrolls, especially the parchments.

—2 Timothy 4:9–13

What do you do when you come to the end of your suffering? How do you walk it through? Where does your longing lie? If you knew, even as the apostle Paul knew, that the fight was almost finished, what would be your final say in the matter?

Paul's final thoughts and finishing desires were rooted in the basics, both in the spiritual and in the physical. Paul would complete his suffering with a final plea for seemingly very little. A final covering that included companionship, a cloak, and some sacred correspondence via his parchments and scrolls.

After a long season of suffering—floggings, imprisonments, shipwrecks, stonings, hunger, nakedness, robbery, shunning from both Jews and Gentiles alike—Paul's short list of wants was reduced to bare essentials. After all, when a soul is exposed in the flesh, when a life is hammered hard and duly stripped of all pretense so that the fake is burned to ashes and the truth smolders in the remains, one is better able to identify what really matters at the end.

I came to understand this more clearly in a season past, when I was given the extraordinary privilege of sitting at the bedside of a dying friend. These would be her final hours; it was evident by her breathing and her seemingly-lessened consciousness of her surroundings. The room was dimly lit, praise and worship music gently serenading the moment.

I was careful to tuck her in, to keep her warm, and to stay close in those moments of fellowship. Softly, I sang the words of "Amazing Grace" in her ear, read to her from God's Holy Word, and then prayed a prayer of gentle release to our Father. I am confident of her participation, because as I readied to leave, I told her that I loved her. Quietly, she mouthed her mirrored response to me.

Twelve hours later, she finished the good fight and entered into her forever and peaceful rest. It was a hard-fought rest on this side of eternity; her suffering was profound. Nonetheless, it was a "difficult" that I am confident she would count as worthy. For to be made whole—to finally see perfection in the eyes of her Father when she exchanged her mortal flesh for her crown and cloaking of final righteousness—is a gift of grace worthy of the journey walked to get there.

Peace in the suffering

We may not be able to see it now, but we will see it then. Some glory is worth our preserving until the end. To receive it all up front—to be relieved from our pain and sufferings in the flesh—is to deny the walk of a crucified life, making our death a moot point, unnecessary and unfinished. The road of suffering is exactly that—a road of final struggling that leads us from our now into our next, to a place of permanence and inexpressible joy.

Accordingly, we cannot deny suffering its portion. As long as we retain the flesh, we retain the need for its removal. From the moment our hearts began beating, we began our walk toward a final surrender. Some will get there quickly; some will come more slowly. Some dressed with a hard suffering; some with a gentler mantle. Still and yet, all will walk it; it is the way of a beating heart.

Better to be covered as we go:

- *With companionship.* With a Luke and a Mark and a Timothy. With those who are willing to walk the road of suffering with us and who choose to enter into our pain because they understand the gift of sacred participation.
- *With a cloaking.* With some warmth and some blankets that wrap their familiar comfort tightly around our flesh, providing us with a momentary pause from the cold and cruelty of a difficult pain.
- *With some correspondence.* With parchments and scrolls. With words upon a page to encourage a weary heart. Words from God, words from friends, and words yet to be written by our own hands.

Paul's final "asking" seems a good covering for a weary suffering. A "getting down to what really matters" as we endeavor to finish our fights well and with a determined resolve that breathes the witness of an intact faith. As we're walking it through and moving toward a better understanding of suffering, material "stuff" isn't the makings of that understanding. It's just filler and always soothes temporarily.

Paul walked his road of suffering with a better comfort—a sacred covering. So did my friend, and by the grace of God, so will I—with a few good companions to encourage me as I go, with the warmth of a favorite cloaking to cover my weariness, and with the truth of God's Word at every turn. That kind of covering, my friends, will carry us far and will finish us home.

In our sufferings and in our pleasure, may we always be so wise as to choose accordingly. Thus, I pray—

Peace for the Journey

Cover us, Lord, with a tender cloaking this day. The world is rife with suffering—in our homes, in our churches, in our schools, in our government. Everywhere we turn, we see the ill effects of what it is to walk this life in the flesh. Humbly, we submit our lives for the road of suffering, and while we long for the release from its constant vigilance, we ask for the grace to walk it when it comes. Give us perspective for our pain. Give us patience for its finish, and grant us peace for the process. You, alone, hold the keys to our peace. You are that peace, Lord. Come and be present amidst our sufferings this day. Amen.

Peace in the suffering

A further pause . . .

- Describe a time of suffering in your own life, whether current or past. What comforts did you cling to? What are you clinging to now during this time? How do these things compare with Paul's list?

- What companions, what cloaking, what words of correspondence do you crave most in your times of suffering?

- Think of a person who has passed from the "now" into the "next" with the same measure of grace and witness as that of my friend. What lasting message did he or she script upon your heart?

- Please read the following scriptures regarding Paul and his suffering. What encouragement or teaching can you glean from his example?

    2 Corinthians 4:16–18

    2 Corinthians 12:1–10

    Philippians 1:12–21

    Philippians 3:7–11

the painful truth

Thomas said to him, "Lord, we don't know where you are going, so how can we know the way?" Jesus answered, "I am the way and the truth and the life. No one comes to the Father except through me."
—John 14:5–6

She cornered me after Bible study last evening. With tears in her eyes, she uttered the pressing concern of her heart. Her question paused my spirit, not because I wasn't prepared for its arrival, but rather because of the pain attached to its asking. It is a pain that often fastens itself to questions that root the deepest—questions that linger hard and long in the murky waters of uncertainties. Questions that surround a soul with a needful longing for clarity. Questions that require our participation because our minds and hearts are equally invested in the answers.

It's not easy to be the recipient of hard questions. Still and yet, it is a privilege to be trusted with their asking, for then we are given the rare opportunity of influence—of speaking something of worth and value into a pain intent on consumption, on paralysis, on keeping a soul from moving beyond its confinement.

That is what I faced last night. It was suffering moment requiring a wisdom beyond my years and limited understanding about why life sometimes seems to portion out raw and rough and rude, almost always with inadequate notice. Her question doesn't breathe in isolation. I've been receiving many of them as of late. They seem to find me, despite my inability to "fix" anything. And last night, as I tossed and turned and tumbled her question over in my mind, I had a thought as it pertains to this "answering" of pain. It has stayed with me throughout the day:

Pain deserves the truth, not preferences.

Read it again, and pause to consider its worth.

Pain deserves the truth, not preferences.

You and I are living in a pain-saturated society. If not our personal pain, then the pain of a people we love—a people we commune with, celebrate life with, go to church with, work with, shop with, "Internet" with, share our resources with, partake in this world with. We are a people living with pain's insistence; and when it comes knocking, it warrants our respect, our notice, and our involvement; It means to claim our participation.

Pain's bang at the door is our invitation to involvement. Rarely do we welcome its intrusion, but almost always are we forced to swallow its intention. Thus, pain deserves more than our menial attempts at soothing. Pain deserves more than our coddling preferences that band-aid

Peace in the suffering

the ache without ever touching the wound. Pain deserves more than our religious speak and our fast-forward approaches to its release.

Pain deserves the truth.

And lest we think that any truth will do—for many are prone to thinking that truth is relative—there is only one truth worthy of a pain's trust, a pain's receiving, and a pain's taking. It is a truth not merely embedded in philosophy. A truth not formulated by man's attempt at having life make sense. A truth not vetted or promoted on the talk show circuit. A truth not rootd in a guru or a mantra or a set of rules for "becoming a better you." None of these "truths" are ample enough, strong enough, steady and sure enough to answer the problem of pain. They fall flat and soothe simplistically and, at the end of the day, inaccurately treat the intrusion of suffering.

Pain deserves better. Pain deserves the truth, not contradictions. Not maybes. Not a "Number One Best-Seller"; but rather, it deserves the certitude and confidence of all creation. Pain deserves the smoldering wick of an eternal flame—a truth that was lit on the front side of Genesis and that continues its watch through until forever. And that truth, my friends, does indeed exist. Truth has a name. It was given to him before the very foundation of the world: *Jesus Christ, Son of the Living God.*

The Word made flesh, living among us for a season, living within us for always through the power of his abiding and Holy Spirit. He is the only truth who is worthy of a pain's holding. He is the only truth who understands the depths of pain's intention.

Thus, when pain finds its way to our doors, the only truth that proves truthful, that remains useful, and that lasts eternal, is the one God who is well familiar with our griefs and our sufferings (Isaiah 53:3). He walked the road of suffering so that we could better walk ours. And if for some reason we think that our road should walk pain free, then we have missed a deeply-rooted tenet of our faith.

Taking up our cross and following after Jesus is to resolutely walk the path of his intention (Luke 9:23–24; 1 Peter 4:12–13). To be like Jesus, we must walk like Jesus. And his walk, fellow pilgrims, was painted with suffering. It was not suffering for suffering's sake, but suffering for our sake, so that when it, too, becomes ours in smaller measure, we will better understand how to walk it through.

God scripts our hearts with a truth that is transparent and real and willing to share in our sufferings. His truth has a purpose that often hides its intention but is, nevertheless, present and profitable for our sacred transformation.

Pain deserves the truth. It deserves our notice, and it deserves our release to the truth. We may never understand pain's grip on this side of eternity. We may never have the perfect words to offer on behalf of pain's intrusion into the lives of others. But if we hold the light of Jesus Christ in our hearts, then we hold more than enough to lead us onward in victory.

Pain doesn't get the final word in our many matters, friends. Neither do our preferences. Truth does. Thus, when pain comes pounding and brings its questions accordingly, may we always find our words and our trust anchored in the Eternal Flame who lights us home and burns us brightly as we go. Thus, I pray—

Seed your Truth within my flesh, Father. Root him deeply and burn him brightly, regardless of the suffering going on around me and in me. Where there are questions, answer them with truth. Where there are tears, dry them with truth. Where there is suffering, cover it with truth, and where there is doubt, replace it with the truth. Keep my heart and my tongue ready with the truth, so that on all occasions your truth stands at the podium and my understanding submits to truth's shadows. May the words of my mouth and the meditations of my heart always be found acceptable in thy sight, O Lord, my Strength, my Redeemer, and my absolute Truth. Amen.

Peace in the suffering

A further pause . . .

- In recent days, what "painful questions" have knocked loudly at the door of your heart?

- How do you deal with painful intrusions? With truth or with coddling preferences? Which is easier for you and why?

- Describe a season where you were forced to deal with pain's intrusion, either your own pain or the pain of another.

- What are some of the sacred "gifts" of pain?

- What do the following scriptures have to say about suffering?

    2 Corinthians 1:3–11

    James 1:2–4

    1 Peter 4:12–13

    1 Peter 5:10

through and through

For Beth, whose faith became sight on July 6, 2009

Test everything. Hold on to the good. Avoid every kind of evil. May God himself, the God of peace, sanctify you through and through. May your whole spirit, soul, and body be kept blameless at the coming of our Lord Jesus Christ. The one who calls you is faithful and he will do it.

—1 Thessalonians 5:21–24

I heard it in her words this morning.

Suffering mingled with faith.

It came to me in the form of an e-mail, anxiously awaiting my notice as I started my day. Words from a friend who is battling for her physical health from a hospital room that's been her home for over a month now. Her life has changed dramatically in that time. She went into surgery with high hopes of gaining some relief from a tumor that was growing on her upper spine. What she received, instead, was partial paralysis in addition to her six-year fight against cancer.

Her hopes have shifted now to include a new focus. Today she lingers with the prospect of a wheelchair and a return home very soon. I imagine it to be enough for her in this moment—to get home to her family and to bask in the warmth of some normalcy, if only for a season.

She's journeying down a long and uncertain road. A "through-and-through" kind of work in her own heart and life that doesn't seem fair. That hardly seems necessary. That rarely feels right and good and pure as it pertains to the life of a saint.

And while I would never want to "explain away her pain" as some part of her purification process—as if there is something in her that needs the lesson of a difficult suffering—I do know this, as it relates to all of us who know Jesus and are walking ever closer to seeing him face-to-face: *Our process of becoming like Jesus is a "through-and-through" kind of process.* It is a word in the Greek language, "holotelous," meaning, "All, or the whole, completely or entirely".[7] The opposite of "holotelous" is "monos," meaning, "only, alone, without others."[8]

Thus, our sanctification is a collective work, not a partial or solitary experience. It is an entire work. A completed work of gathering experiences that can only be accomplished through the faithful hands of a peaceful God. He seeds our lives with the continual flames of a holy fire and with his holy end in mind. He is a God who is after far more in us and through us than we are willing to concede at the time of our salvation.

Peace in the suffering

Surrendering our hearts to the way of the cross is a costly decision. It means that we willingly submit our flesh to the purifying flames of a holier notion—a better becoming that remains unfinished should we choose to stay as we are rather than become who we are meant to be.

When we say "yes" to Jesus and his cross, we say "yes" to our Father's "through-and-through." Rarely do we understand on the front side of our "yes" what that will look like in the seasons to come. A good "ignorance," I suppose. God grows us in our sanctification. To receive it all in our first encounter of knowing Jesus would be too much. Perhaps, it would be too hard, too difficult a cloaking at the moment when our tender hearts make the decision to cross the line from flesh to faith.

A "through-and-through" kind of work is a gift from a gracious God who realizes that the more we grow in our understanding of just exactly how long and wide and high and deep his blood was shed on our behalf, the more willing we become to concede our flesh for the same. When we finally arrive at the place of fully perceiving Christ's love for us, then we are willing, like the apostle Paul, to surrender it all—our flesh and our now—for the sake of our completed end.

It's not easy. It's not always fun. It's never predictable, and rarely does it ever make sense. But in God's hands and through God's love, of this one truth we can be sure: *It is always good.* It is always right, and his work in us is always for us, for him, and for a kingdom's sake that exceeds our momentary grasp at understanding.

There is coming a day when our "through-and-through" will make it through to the other side. God will push our flesh through an invisible barrier, and in a moment's pause, our faith will be made sight. We will have the glorious truth of our difficult "now" laid out before us in a way that makes perfect sense and that will leave us panting a breathless "hallelujah" for the process we've walked to get there.

Hold onto the good, weary pilgrims. Hold onto the promise. His name is Jesus, and he is faithful to complete in us that which he began over two thousand years ago on a hillside named Calvary. Perfection. A "faultless-to-stand-before-the-throne" kind of finish because of his willingness to bow before the throne on a cross.

Oh, what wondrous love is this! It is a love that calls us to a "through-and-through" kind of faith. May we all have the good sense and the willing "yes" in our hearts to take up our cross and follow faith through to the threshold of our finish that will birth the truth of our beginning again.

Peace for the Journey

It is a beginning that lands us safely at home, at rest, and face-to-face with the God who created us with such sacred splendor in mind. Thus, I pray—

Carry us through to our completion, Lord. Let not our temporary ills be a stumbling block in our understanding of your perfect intention for our end. You are that end, Father. Keep us to it all the days of our lives, with a wisdom that exceeds sense, with a patience that exceeds the pain, and with a hope that surpasses the heartache that forces our faith and that weakens our resolve. Through and through, home to you. Grant us your grace for the journey. Amen.

Peace in the suffering

A further pause . . .

- Consider some moments in your life that have required a "through-and-through" kind of faith. Describe.

- Looking back and looking within, how did God shape your heart and your faith toward a more perfect understanding of him? What did you learn about God in that season? What did you learn about yourself?

- Jesus had a life laced with "through-and-through" moments. Read about one of them in Matthew 26:36–56. How was Christ's suffering mingled with a tenacious and absolute faith?

- Purposefully consider areas in your own life in need of a deeper perfection. Write out a prayer to our Father, surrendering your need and receiving his strength and peace for the sanctifying to come.

6
Peace in the mountains

You will bring them in and plant them on the mountain of your inheritance—the place, O LORD, you made for your dwelling, the sanctuary, O Lord, your hands established.

—Exodus 15:17

a peaked perspective

> *The LORD descended to the top of Mount Sinai and called Moses to the top of the mountain. So Moses went up.*
>
> —Exodus 19:20

Do you know why I love the mountains? Because on God's mountains the air is lighter, the view is better, and the heavens are closer.

Carved in splendor and crowned with the beauty of God's creative genius, mountains are the silent sanctuaries of sacred worship that chorus the praise of seasoned thankfulness. In the blossom of spring, in the shade of summer, in the colors of fall, in the barren of winter, in all seasons, mountains house the magnificent, living witness of a Father's loving embrace.

Perhaps this is why it is easy for me to find my God in the mountains. Whether viewing them from a distance or actually ascending their terrain for a closer look, mountains house God's language of invitation—to come. To climb. To awaken and to find the fellowship and presence of the God who inhabits his hills with a seemingly holy preference.

Mountains continue to be the venue in which sacred moments are birthed in the hearts of those who are willing to embrace the ascent. Good stuff surfaces in God's mountains; thus, my appreciation for the occasions that afford me such a growing.

When we allow our walks a pause to behold the splendor of a mountain moment with God, he is faithful to bear witness with our obedience to ascend. God created his mountains with the view in mind. He intends for us to climb into his presence and to open up our eyes to envision the beauty of the landscape below. When we do, we better understand the sacred worth of such a moment. We capture it and bottle it deep within, keeping careful guard to make sure we aren't robbed of its remembrance.

Mountaintop moments are the stuff of kingdom living. Without them, the walk in the valley below steps hard and empty and void of hope. Without the witness of God's presence in our lives, there is no calm in our chaos, no substance in our steps, no peace in our journeys. We wander aimlessly with the shadow of a telling nothingness.

If we never take the occasion to "go up" *to* God, we will never behold the beauty of a "looking down" *with* God. Being able to look down into the world with God's perspective is the reward that is birthed from rich intimacy with him.

Peace in the mountains

Moses' life was crowned with many mountaintop moments. He had the rare privilege of climbing into the literal presence of God on several occasions, seeding his heart for a consecrated obedience:

- A burning bush kind of moment: "'Do not come any closer,' God said. 'Take off your sandals, for the place where you are standing is holy ground'" (Exodus 3:5).
- A Ten Commandments kind of moment: "When the LORD finished speaking to Moses on Mount Sinai, he gave him the two tablets of the Testimony, the tablets of stone inscribed by the finger of God" (Exodus 31:18).
- A sacred radiance kind of moment: "When Moses came down from Mount Sinai with the two tablets of the Testimony in his hands, he was not aware that his face was radiant because he had spoken with the LORD" (Exodus 34:29).
- A view of the Promised Land kind of moment: "Then Moses climbed Mount Nebo from the plains of Moab to the top of Pisgah, across from Jericho. There the LORD showed him the whole land. . . . Then the LORD said to him, 'This is the land I promised on oath to Abraham, Isaac and Jacob when I said, "I will give it to your descendants." I have let you see it with your eyes, but you will not cross over into it'" (Deuteronomy 34:1, 4).
- An entering into his eternal rest kind of moment: "And Moses the servant of the LORD died there in Moab, as the LORD had said. He buried him in Moab" (Deuteronomy 34:5–6).

Indeed, sacred moments for Moses. No wonder he climbed. No wonder he obeyed. Who of us doesn't want the same? What valley could we walk that would warrant the neglect of such holy occasions? What refusal could we offer that would seem sensible? Why would we forsake the splendor of a mountain view in favor of flat and monotonous living? Why, indeed, when our Father has issued his summons to us to come and to feast in his presence?

This is not just on special occasions or as we happen upon them while "driving thru." But rather, each and every day, because his invitation is an every-day kind of offer. We are the privileged children of God. We have our Father's lap and our Father's love as our eternal wrapping. We need not linger any further at the base of his mountain. We simply need to "climb up" to our "bowing down"—the one posture that always precedes the sacred splendor of a mountain view.

Thank God for his mountains and for such moments. We need his burning bushes and his holy Word, his sacred radiance and his view of our Promised Land. Greater still, we need the gift of his eternal and lasting rest—the burial of our flesh through the nail-scarred hands of his surrender. Such a treasure allows us to walk down from our mountains with the hope of glory hidden in our hearts and bursting forth through our countenance.

Good stuff—God's stuff—is ready for the unveiling as we pilgrim to the place of his high and holy preference. It is a portion of sacred ground, where the air breathes lighter, the view visions better, and the heavens are as close as our next breath. Thus, I pray—

Onward and upward, Father, I come to your mountain. Not because you don't walk the valley with me, but simply because the ascent affords me a better view—an eternal perspective that strengthens my steps for the seasons when my vision is limited. Thank you for the moments of sacred intimacy that come with the climb and with the lingering in your presence once I arrive. Give me the endurance to make the journey, wisdom to know when I am in need of such a pilgrimage, and the humility to bow in your presence. I am grateful for the climb that always yields the faithful fruit of unseen vistas. Amen.

A further pause . . .

- Recall a favorite mountaintop moment you've shared with God. What made it special, and what sacred vision did you carry with you as you descended from that moment?

- Moses experienced many mountaintop moments with God. Of the five listed above, which one would you most like to experience in coming days? Why?

- Describe one or two other occasions in Scripture where mountain encounters revealed deep communion with God?

- Why do you think that God often chooses the mountains as his place of holy dwelling?

 *keepers of the light*

There the angel of the LORD appeared to him in the flames of fire from within a bush. Moses saw that though the bush was on fire it did not burn up. So Moses thought, "I will go over and see this strange sight—why the bush does not burn up." When the LORD saw that he had gone over to look, God called to him from within the bush, "Moses! Moses!" And Moses said, "Here I am."

—Exodus 3:2–3

I am drawn to fire.

Be it through the single flame of a candle or the collective kindling of a winter's hearth, a fire calls for my notice and beckons my participation. Partly because of its beauty. Partly because of its warmth. But mainly because of the inherent power contained within its blaze. It is a power that, if not restrained, will quickly leap boundaries and consume surroundings.

Fire possesses the strength to force change and to alter a forever. Fire grabs the attention of the curious and begs their approach for a closer look. Within such closeness, the heat is felt and kindles the light of another wick, a heart that was meant to flame with the power of a consuming God. He calls us to be his torchbearers in a world longing for the fire's warmth.

Moses noticed the fire. In the midst of his "normal," his eyes fixed upon the abnormal—a burning bush that flamed with furious intention, all the while refusing the fire's consumption. Moses could have moved his "normal" to another location, could have taken pasture on another mountain, but he didn't. Instead of shuffling away from danger, Moses chose to draw close to its perimeter. Once there, he felt the flames of an eternal calling that would consume his heart and kindle his forever.

There is much we can learn from Moses about God's kindling of a sacred fire.

God lit the fire. Moses acknowledged its presence.

All around us, each and every day, fires burn. Most burn with the flames of our daily routine—flames that could all too quickly consume our every moment if not for our watchful gaze. But there are other fires that burn with abnormality—sacred flames from God's purposeful intent. Too often they go unnoticed because we are too busy putting out the fires of routine. The key lies in discerning which fires are worthy of our pause and, therefore, worthy of our Father's fanning them into brighter flame.

God stood within the fire. Moses approached its perimeter.

Fires worthy of our approach are those containing the presence of God. How do we know the difference? We look for flames rather than ashes. We pay attention to the fires that burn with intensity, fires that remain. Temporal fires can be quenched by temporal means. Sacred fires can never be quenched. They burn with the heat of eternity and are meant to fuel our desire for God.

Is there a fire in your life right now that won't go away? A burning bush that is flaming with increasing intensity rather than diminishing to embers? Perhaps God is calling for your approach to its perimeter. Only by moving closer will you be able to hear him calling your name.

God spoke from the fire. Moses accepted his proclamation.

God never forces our approach to his sacred flames. But once we arrive in obedience, he is quick to offer his calling. Like Moses, we should be quick to offer our "here I am."

God looks for our approach, for our desire and our willingness to entreat his extraordinary masking—a sacred fire that never grows dim, never breathes cold, and never burns to ashes. With its embrace, we hear our names spoken from the lips of our Father, who has ordained our lives for the kindling of his mighty purposes. It is a sacred calling that we cannot afford to miss.

And so this day, like Moses, let us *acknowledge the fire's presence* in our lives. Let us *approach its perimeter* with cautious pause, and with holy fear and a portion of sacred trembling, let us *accept its proclamation*. God's sacred fires surround our every day. Our future is shaped by our embrace or neglect of their warmth.

My own life has recently known the interruption of a burning bush that required my acknowledgement. In faith, I began my approach to its heat; the closer I came, the clearer my Father's voice as he called my name. I have accepted his summons, but not without some reservations.

Am I scared? A little, but what scares me the most is what I stand to miss by not approaching the flames of God's calling. I don't want to forsake the sound of my name falling from the lips of my Father's divine intent. I don't want to miss the fire's kindling for the sake of preserving my "normal."

Neither do you, for with the fire comes a life as it was meant to burn—with passionate purpose and a power that cannot be contained. Thus, I pray—

Burn us Father, with the sacred flames of your intent. Give us the eyes to acknowledge your presence. Give us the courage to approach your perimeter. And when our knees bow in humble submission, give us the clarity to accept the proclamation of our calling. To go and make disciples. To go and proclaim the truth. To go and kindle the flame of another wick that longs to burn with the intensity of your sacred heat. Humbly I ask. Readily I receive my calling to be a keeper of your light. Amen.

A further pause . . .

- When have you, like Moses, experienced a "burning bush" kind of moment with God? Describe.

- Consider Moses' three-fold response to God's fire as it pertains to your own burning bush moment: acknowledging its presence, approaching its perimeter, accepting its proclamation.

- Were you able to walk the process through to the end? Which step caused you the most difficulty?

- What has been the resulting outcome of your "burning bush"?

- In what current situation in your life would you most like to see the witness of God's burning bush and his voice? Tell him about it. Ask him for it, and then receive your Father's warmth as he is faithful to present himself within the approaching flames.

Peace in the mountains

 a worthy climb

> *And God sent an angel to destroy Jerusalem. But as the angel was doing so, the Lord saw it and was grieved because of the calamity and said to the angel who was destroying the people, "Enough! Withdraw your hand." The angel of the Lord was then standing at the threshing floor of Araunah the Jebusite.*
> —1 Chronicles 21:15

The threshing floor.

A hardened surface used in ancient times for the spreading out of wheat so that the edible grain could be loosened from the inedible chaff.

Cutting through the chaff to get to the palatable continues to be a critical step in the harvesting process. Without the grain's release from its hardened casing, the ripened seeds are reduced in their usefulness. Rather than baking to bread, they are assigned as fodder for livestock or buried as waste beneath a soil's re-tilling. When the grain refuses its necessary pounding, the grain evades its intended purpose.

As it goes with wheat, so it goes with the history of mankind. God is a thresher of wheat as it pertains to the life of his people. He is after our usefulness and will do what is necessary to cut through our chaff to get to the edible. He isn't content to leave us in our current condition; instead, God's intention has always been to make us into something more . . .

His.

Getting there sometimes requires the pain of a holy threshing on the hardened surface of a hardened will. King David underwent such a threshing. This man after God's own heart knew a lifetime of shaping beneath the winnowing fork of his Father's intention. Those of us on a similar quest can count on the same. Our threshing may not look exactly like David's, but it sometimes feels comparable in its depth.

King David's refinement would take place on a mountain. As Christians, we usually associate mountain moments with times of intimate exchange with the presence of Almighty God, and rightly so, because Scripture is replete with the connection. Mountains, both then and now, serve as God's invitation for humanity to climb into his presence and to view the world from a higher perspective. And while not all mountain moments are laced with the difficulty of David's encounter, mountain moments with God are always confrontational, intended to bring about a change of heart.

David's change of heart was a necessary one. Behind him? Three days of punishment from the sword of the Lord, costing the lives of seventy thousand Israelites. David's sin—counting his army's strength in numbers rather than counting on the strength of his God—was the culprit behind the carnage. It was a high price to pay on the front side of a mountain climb, yet one that was allowed King David so that when he received the summons to "go up" he was more than ready to comply with the ascent.

His climb climaxed at the threshing floor of Araunah. David built an altar and offered a sacrifice in hopes of assuaging his Father's wrath. It cost David. True sacrifice always comes with a price tag. Not because our God is trying to bleed us dry, but rather because he is worthy of a lavish surrender.

David let go of the temporal in order to take hold of the eternal. Six hundred golden shekels and a few sacrifices later, God's sword of vengeance found its sheath as his fire found its kindling upon David's altar. A threshing floor on a mountain where David would proclaim, "The house of the LORD God is to be here, and also the altar of burnt offering for Israel" (1 Chronicles 22:1).

Read that again slowly, and let it sink deeply—"The house of the LORD God, and also the burnt offering for Israel."

This was no accidental climb for King David. This was a moment of divine, sacred planning, written into the script long before he would ascend to its holiness. David's son, King Solomon, would build that house—the temple of the Lord, where the ark of the covenant would find its rest on a floor that once threshed wheat. A place where, nearly a thousand years later, another threshing would take place.

God's edible grain, Jesus Christ, would take a willing pounding to be loosened from his fleshly casing in order to become the intended purpose of his Father's heart—the Bread of Life. It was a feeding that cost God dearly—the life of his only Son. Jesus didn't forego his threshing because he understood the value of what was at stake should he walk away . . .

Us.

Thus, he willingly made the ascent to the threshing floor of Calvary and surrendered his body upon the altar of burnt offering in order to fulfill his sacred purpose. In doing so, he enabled us to fulfill ours.

Sometimes there comes a threshing that calls for a mountain's climb—a moment worthy of the arduous ascent because of the One who is waiting for us at the top. And when we get there, when we fall into the arms of our Father and consider the view from his perspective, we won't have to wonder if the climb was worth it or not. His climb or ours. In that moment, we will behold the visible truth—a backward glance that validates and authenticates every hard-fought step of a difficult obedience.

Peace in the mountains

Climbing into the presence of Jesus to be more like Jesus is always a worthy climb. A worthy forever. Thus, I pray—

Keep us to our climbing, Father, toward your presence and in the sacred truth of a mountain's pause. When our feet grow weary and we cannot vision the worth of the ascent, bolster our steps with the promise of unseen vistas and longed for moments with you. Today, I submit my heart for the harvesting and the threshing that leads me onward and upward into your eternal rest. You, alone, are worthy of the ascent. Keep my focus steady until I see you face-to-face and walk with you in the mountain home that you've prepared for me. Amen.

Peace for the Journey

A further pause . . .

- When have you known the difficulty of a mountain's climb to get to God's presence?

- What were your reasons for making the journey?

- Read the full account of today's Scripture focus found in 1 Chronicles 21; picture the scene in vivid detail as you read.

- What was Araunah's offering to David in verse 23? What was David's response to that offering in verses 24–25? What was God's response to David's offering in verse 26? What does this description of threshing/sacrifice have to teach us about our own pilgrimage of surrender?

- You are the dwelling place of the Most High God. You don't have to climb a literal mountain to get to his presence. You simply have to build an altar within your heart. Take time today to build that altar with your personal stones of surrender. Go up to God. He is waiting to meet with you even now.

Peace in the mountains

 packing up a vacation, punctuating a week

You will go out in joy and be led forth in peace; the mountains and hills will burst into song before you, and all the trees of the field will clap their hands.
—Isaiah 55:12

I was ready to come home. Vacation is always a mixed bag of everything for me. Good, along with the bad, and a whole lot of other that rests in between.

I was tired going into our trip. I am even more tired coming out of it, and even now, I can barely muster the strength for a complete thought. But there is a lingering pause—one final memory of our time in the Smoky Mountains worthy of my pen tonight.

Trees.

I spent some time with them yesterday afternoon. A storm was brewing—the kind of storm that smells before it swells. I knew my moments of outdoor devotion would be brief. I'm not a storm girl. They frighten me, but yesterday I found my strength in their embrace. I grabbed my Bible and headed out to the deck of our mountain loft. The hot and humid June afternoon gave way to the cool breeze of a better wind.

And despite my chaotic emotions, God used his trees to teach me a few things about clutter-free living. Things like:

- *Trees are rooted for the wind.* Rarely, if ever, do they break with the wind's embrace. Instead, they are quick to bow in welcome surrender.
- *Trees are the instruments of the wind.* When the force of a wind caresses the limbs of its instrument, the melody is magical.
- *Trees move in rhythm with the wind.* They don't bobble and bumble their way through the song. They sway in step with their conductor.
- *Trees bend with the wind,* for the touching forth and the falling back and the rebounding home to center.
- *Trees are content to share the stage with the wind's choice of companions.* Rarely are their songs a solo act. Their brothers and sisters are often called upon to add their voices.
- *Trees sing regardless of the wind.* Each and every spring they burst onto the scene, budded with new life. Each and every fall, they hide with the barren prospect of a winter's calling. In season and out, trees are steadfast and true. They do not worry

about a spring's budding or a fall's stripping. They simply are. They trust God for the song.
- *Trees have longevity, despite the wind.* They've been around for a long time. They were the pronounced goodness of a Father's third day extravaganza. They will follow us all the way to heaven.
- *Trees submit to the wind,* not begrudgingly, but with the bending and blending of voices singing a perfect song to the God who made them for his renown because . . .
- *Trees understand that their voices sing because of the wind.* Left in stillness, their song remains silent. With the wind, they are stirred toward a richer refrain.

Trees and wind. Sometimes, an unwelcome coupling. To the novice—to those untrained in the melodies of creation—a tree's rustling sounds like little more than the approach of an oncoming storm. But to me, a lover of creation and one in search of the sacred song, the rhythm of the trees sounds like the refrain of heaven.

In the pause of yesterday's shower, I was reminded that there is song that exists apart from me. A song that is sung, sometimes, in spite of me. A song that will continue to sing, not because of me, but because of the Creator who commissioned its voice for such adoration.

Trees do not sing for man's approval. They simply sing because our Father has given them the voice to do so. And on the eve of a vacation's ending, I stepped away from my routine to participate in the chorus of the divine.

It is a song that never grows old. A song that always sings pure. A song that fully and most assuredly breathes grace. And even though I'm home now, if I listen intently, close my eyes and focus tightly, I can hear the rustling melody of my Father's kingdom chorus as I walk my way to sleep.

What a perfectly satisfying way to pack up my vacation and punctuate my week atop God's mountains. Thus, I pray—

Thank you, Father, for the chorus of your creation that bursts onto my scene and begs for my notice. Open my eyes to see the beauty of your handiwork. Open my ears to hear the chorus of your melody. Open my mouth to taste the flavors of your goodness. Open my senses to feel and to smell the splendor of your creative genius, and open my heart to receive the fullness of your presence. When I forget to sing your praises, Lord, stir your trees in my absence. Let all creation voice the truth of who you are. Amen.

A further pause . . .

- Describe a time when you witnessed the trees dancing in rhythm with the wind's embrace. What, if any, part of the dance spoke an eternal truth beyond what your eyes could see?

- Compare your response to a "windy storm" with a tree's response. In what way is your response similar? Different?

- Read Psalm 96 aloud, keeping the sound of the swaying trees as your accompaniment. What part of creation most clearly follows through with God's command to "sing" as described in this Psalm?

- Consider a tree's response to seasons: spring, summer, fall, and winter. Describe. Which one of the seasonal trees most accurately depicts your current season of living?

 *proximity to presence*

> *There he went into a cave and spent the night. And the word of the LORD came to him: "What are you doing here?" He replied, "I have been very zealous for the LORD God Almighty. The Israelites have rejected your covenant, broken down your altars, and put your prophets to death with the sword. I am the only one left, and now they are trying to kill me too." The LORD said, "Go out and stand on the mountain in the presence of the LORD, for the LORD is about to pass you by."*
>
> —1 Kings 19:9–11

There is a lie that is being spread about me—an untruth that levels as detrimental to the cause of Jesus Christ. It bites hard and spreads its poison into the life-giving vein that cannot abide both the eternal truth and the lie's lethal venom.

It's probably been said about you before. You've probably even said it about yourself. Most of us wear it without ever realizing it. We carry it around as our truth, and in so doing, it becomes rich fodder for water cooler conversations—hell's conversation. Our acceptance of the venom fuels the fire and stokes the flames of an enemy's malicious intent to steal, kill, and destroy.

The lie?

I am the *only one*.

No, I am not. Neither are you; still and yet, we pride ourselves on thinking we walk in isolation with the sufferings and grievances that set us apart as extraordinary and worthy of a gracious pity. We lick our wounds and salve our difficulties with self-talk that defeats rather than uplifts. That shackles rather than frees. That limits rather than unleashes.

We are not the only ones who have . . .

- had a bad day;
- been financially reduced;
- been ignored by a lover;
- been ignored by a crowd;
- passed over for a job promotion;
- felt isolated in a sea of siblings;
- felt isolated as an only child;
- suffered in the flesh;
- known the crush of defeat;
- known the depth of rejection;
- felt the heat of unwarranted flames;
- been disappointed by humanity;

Peace in the mountains

- experienced the struggle of a waiting dream;
- watched a prodigal child continue in his or her rebellion;
- buried a child, a parent, a spouse, a friend;
- felt the crushing blow of sin's depth;
- felt the weight of condemnation, even after the grip of redemption;
- _____ .

We may feel like we are the only ones, but the truth is, we have never been the only ones.

There is another who has walked the breadth of understanding on our behalf. And because of his willingness to do so, he is tendered by our struggle and calls us to his presence for a better perspective, a holier truth, one that is not applied with the wind or an earthquake or even with the purifying flames of a consecrated fire. But rather, one that is salved through the gentle whisper of a Father who bends to ask, "What are you doing here?"

God's question requires a prior submission. It requires a hard and deliberate obedience that walks through difficult terrain in order to reach his tabernacled presence. Making the ascent to God's dwelling is our necessary compliance for receiving the healing perspective that voices the truer truth—we are not alone. Our God is with us, even to the end of the age (Matthew 28:20).

Elijah came to Mt. Horeb to receive this perspective. Wearied by his flight, his fear, his exhaustion, and his "lack and seemingly little," he pilgrimed the forty-day journey to arrive at the one place he knew he would find safety. He climbed into the cleft of God's rock, where he found rest and witnessed the tender passing by of his Father's presence.

A mountaintop moment if ever there was one. A gentle whisper of grace was granted to this servant who, despite his heaviness of heart and fragility of frame, understood that finding God's peace would require his willingness to put movement behind his desire. To put faith ahead of his feelings, and to put pursuit of the truth ahead of the paralyzing lie that sought to keep him as he was—alone and defeated.

Elijah moved forward to God's mountain because he understood that proximity births presence.

Every time. Not only in moments of raw desperation that force the matter, but in moments of usual routine and everyday living, when the need seems less insistent but, nevertheless, just as necessary. Whenever you and I take the occasion to move into a place of worship with Jesus—when we move our hearts within close proximity to his—he is faithful to meet us with the gentle witness of his presence and with the whispers of the truest truth. It is a truth that speaks "community" over the lie of the *only one*.

God has reserved a remnant of people, like you, whose knees bow only to him. They, too, are walking a difficult journey, in search of peace and with the hope of finding God's presence. Your life doesn't exist in isolation. You may feel as if it does, perhaps even in this moment. But you are not the only one. You are part of a great cloud of witnesses who have gone before, who stand with you now, and who will follow in your shadow.

Even if no one surfaces to pilgrim alongside you in the flesh, your Father is there, deep within your heart and companioning your steps all the way home to him. If Jesus is your Savior, then you have proximity to his presence every moment of your life. Getting to him doesn't require an arduous climb up Mt. Horeb. Getting to him simply requires an inward intention to do so. To pause from the ordinary and to listen for the extraordinary whispers of God, who is faithful to voice his witness as we are faithful in our drawing close to listen.

Whether it comes in the wind or an earthquake, in the fire or a gentle breeze, God's truth is an enabling truth. It fosters a sacred rest, a needed healing, and a perfect peace—all of which fortify our flesh and our faith for the journey ahead. For a walk back down that mountain with the facts in hand and with the whisper of his presence protecting our hearts as we go. Thus, I pray—

> *When I am tempted with the lie that "I am the only one," remind me of your presence, Lord. Forgive me for simple-minded thinking that isolates rather than communicates. Bring me into a fuller understanding of your tabernacled existence within my feeble flesh. Give me the wisdom to conceive it, the faith to believe it, and the strength to breathe it every day of my life. I am not the only one; I stand with the One, with you, Father, as I walk this journey in joyful expectation of the day when I ascend that final mountain to my forever. Amen.*

Peace in the mountains

A further pause . . .

- When have you felt like "the only one"? Fill in the blank with your own labels: "I am the only one who _____."

- In this current moment, how would you answer God's question to Elijah: "What are you doing here?"

- Take time to read 1 Kings 19:9–18. Consider a time in your own life when you felt the sure presence of God. How did he arrive—in a wind, earthquake, fire, or whisper? Describe.

- What are some tangible steps you can take to foster further proximity to God's presence in your every day?

7
Peace at church

For where two or three come together in my name, there am I with them.

—Matthew 18:20

 *posturing our hearts for a sabbath rest*

Thus the heavens and the earth were completed in all their vast array. By the seventh day God had finished the work he had been doing; so on the seventh day he rested from all his work. And God blessed the seventh day and made it holy, because on it he rested from all the work of creating that he had done.

—Genesis 2:1–3

It's coming around again. An ending to a week that's just barely begun. I couldn't have accurately forecasted its path seven days ago because chaotic living is my norm. Most weeks spend as a blur, and by week's end, exhaustion finds its bed within my weary frame.

I am tired, and I am in need.

My Father knows my requirement, and thus he gives me permission for a Sabbath pause—a gift of rest that is consecrated and set apart for my ceasing from the ordinary in order to partake of the extraordinary.

The problem? I rarely take the time to open his gift, and tonight I ponder the probable cause behind my denial.

The Israelites got caught up within the particulars of a Sabbath's rest. Regulations and requisites ruled the day. As is so often the case, whenever the law of religion supersedes the grace of its faith, rest is rarely found.

I am afraid that we are not so far in our thinking and in our doing from our spiritual ancestors. We busy ourselves with the many details of a Sabbath observance. Church life requires it. We didn't mean for it to be this way, to make Sundays a day of work rather than a day of rest. It is simply the nature of the beast that we have amply fed with our programs and perfections.

Instead of entering into the gift of God's rest, we exhaust ourselves by walking around it—coddling it with the promise of our return once the details have walked their course. Unfortunately, the details are often many, and their pace is measured by the cadence of man's intent rather than the consecration of God's endowment.

We have made the Sabbath a difficult embrace. God has always intended it for our simple acceptance. Tonight I am wondering what it would take for us to arrive at a similar conclusion—to get to the point where we lay down our frenetic lifestyle in exchange for a posture that simply lies down.

Not long ago, God painted a portrait of rest for me. He did so through the nesting of some newborn robins that were gathered in the refuge of a front door's, hanging wreath. Momma robin was absent, allowing me a closer peek at her offspring. I watched them huddle closely together, hemmed in by the twigs and leaves that she had carefully selected as their shelter. Their fragile necks strained in expectation of her return to the nest. Instinctively, they seemed to understand that her arrival would provide them with sustenance to feed their hunger. I don't imagine they worried about much else beyond their need to be fed. They simply gathered together in anticipation of what was to come. The robins have much to teach us about a Sabbath pause, for they have perfected a consecrated rest.

A Sabbath rest is found in the hiding:

- "For in the day of trouble he will keep me safe in his dwelling; he will hide me in the shelter of his tabernacle and set me high upon a rock" (Psalm 27:5).
- "He will cover you with his feathers, and under his wings you will find refuge; his faithfulness will be your shield and rampart" (Psalm 91:4).

A Sabbath rest is found in the sheltering with brothers and sisters:

- "Let us not give up meeting together, as some are in the habit of doing, but let us encourage one another—and all the more as you see the Day approaching" (Hebrews 10:25).
- "Every day they continued to meet together in the temple courts. They broke bread in their homes and ate together with glad and sincere hearts, praising God and enjoying the favor of all the people. And the Lord added to their number daily those who were being saved" (Acts 2:46–47).

A Sabbath rest is found in the lifting up of heads:

- "I lift up my eyes to the hills—where does my help come from? My help comes from the LORD, the Maker of heaven and earth" (Psalm 121:1–2).
- "But you are a shield around me, O LORD; you bestow glory on me and lift up my head. To the LORD I cry aloud, and he answers me from his holy hill" (Psalm 3:3–4).

A Sabbath rest is found in the waiting:

- "Yet the LORD longs to be gracious to you; he rises to show you compassion. For the LORD is a God of justice. Blessed are all who wait for him!" (Isaiah 30:18).
- "I waited patiently for the LORD; he turned to me and heard my cry" (Psalm 40:1).

A Sabbath rest is found in an open mouth:

- "I am the LORD your God, who brought you out of Egypt. Open wide your mouth and I will fill it" (Psalm 81:10).
- "The Sovereign LORD has given me an instructed tongue, to know the word that sustains the weary. He wakens me morning by morning, wakens my ear to listen like one being taught" (Isaiah 50:4).

A Sabbath rest is found in the filling:

- "Let them give thanks to the LORD for his unfailing love and his wonderful deeds for men, for he satisfies the thirsty and fills the hungry with good things" (Psalm 107:9).
- "Then Jesus declared, 'I am the bread of life. He who comes to me will never go hungry, and he who believes in me will never be thirsty'" (John 6:35).

A Sabbath rest is found in an eventual launching:

- "Therefore go and make disciples of all nations, baptizing them in the name of the Father and of the Son and of the Holy Spirit, and teaching them to obey everything I have commanded you. And surely I am with you always, to the very end of the age" (Matthew 28:19–20).

Hiding. Sheltering. Lifting. Waiting. Opening. Filling. Launching. The posture of a Sabbath rest. Not requirements and regulations. Simply a lying down for a day so that a rising up for tomorrow can find its wings and take flight.

I am tired, friends, and I am in need. How about you? How long has it been since you've known a Sabbath's rest? Would you allow the robins, along with the Word of God, to be the compass that leads you there this weekend? Next week belongs to next. God's Sabbath belongs to our today; thus, I pray—

Take us there, Lord, to a place of rest and consecration underneath the shelter of your wings. Surround us with the care and comfort of your people as we rest. Lift our heads from our temporal and focus our eyes on your eternal. Teach us the patience of a sacred waiting. Feed us, Father, for we are hungry for your Word. Fill us, Jesus, for you alone can satisfy the craving of our souls. And when our rest is full and finished—complete and more than enough—breathe your breath to launch us into a world that needs to find its sacred pause. Amen.

Peace at church

A further pause . . .

- Why is it so difficult to host a Sabbath rest?

- Why is it necessary?

- Review the robin family's posture of rest and the corresponding scriptures regarding hiding, sheltering, lifting, waiting, opening, filling, launching. Where does the breakdown happen for you?

- Be intentional about finding your Sabbath rest this week; it's our Father's very good gift to you. Spend it with him. Journal some specific ways you can be more deliberate about opening God's gift.

 ## *sacramental second helpings*

> *People were bringing little children to Jesus to have him touch them, but the disciples rebuked them. When Jesus saw this, he was indignant. He said to them, "Let the little children come to me, and do not hinder them, for the kingdom of God belongs to such as these. I tell you the truth, anyone who will not receive the kingdom of God like a child will never enter it." And he took the children in his arms, put his hands on them and blessed them.*
>
> —Mark 10:13–16

I think perhaps I broke ranks with religious protocol yesterday. Somewhere between singing "If You're Happy and You Know It" and the final prayers of a children's church hour, there came an unscripted moment that would cause me to ponder the "rules of engagement" for doing this thing called "church."

Yesterday we celebrated the sacrament of Holy Communion in our congregation. Per custom, the bread and juice were brought to the children who were participating in worship in another location. It was my turn on the rotation as their teacher, and therefore, I would be responsible for administering the "elements" to these formative young minds. With our time quickly drawing to a close, I ushered the children from the craft area back to our worship area, where we paused to consider the sacrament.

The bread and wine. The representative body and blood of our Lord Jesus Christ. A last supper between friends. A time of mingling grief for the journey ahead. A sacred pause in the life of the one known as Master, Teacher, Fisherman, and Friend. A taste of the Divine as it lingered in their mouths and transformed their souls. Communion. Fellowship. Holy remembrance. These were the "elements" of the story I had the privilege of sharing with the impressionable minds of a dozen youth prior to their partaking of them.

Whether or not they fully grasped the significance of the moment, they were more than ready to grasp the provision of the moment. One by one they came, carefully dipping the small piece of bread into the cup and hearing these words spoken on their behalf, "The body and blood of Christ, shed for you," on down the line until every mouth was filled. Everyone wanted to partake, and then to my surprise, all wanted to partake again.

Not sure how to respond to their requests for "second helpings," I simply went with the moment and emphatically said "yes." It didn't take long for the plate to be wiped clean by little hands eager for more of this sacred sustenance. They giggled with glee, and I laughed with joy as we all shouted between bites, "We remember you, Jesus, we remember you!"

Peace at church

Indeed, the sacrament of communion was celebrated in our time of worship together. I'm not sure what drove a dozen kids to want more of the elements. The practice of communion births an intrigue all its own. And while others might not appreciate my willingness to let them partake of second helpings, I believe that Jesus approved.

In a few moments of Sabbath rest, God used his little children to script a sacred metaphor for anyone who is willing to look beyond the rituals of faith to understand what it means to be in relationship with the Author of that faith. And just as children sometimes rob us of our pretense and protocol in worship, so it was for a group of young hearts over two thousand years ago who stepped all over protocol to simply get a taste of their Father.

Jesus was in town. His reputation arrived ahead of him, stirring the people to come and get a closer look at this Nazarene who authored miracles and taught the truth of the Scriptures with eloquent expertise. The gospel of Mark records that, "People were bringing little children to Jesus to have him touch them, but the disciples rebuked them."

The Greek transliterated word for touch is "hapto," meaning, "to fasten to, adhere to; to fasten fire to a thing, kindle, set on fire."[9] People were bringing their children to God's lap in hopes that he would fasten, adhere, and kindle the divine spark of himself into their very being.

Unfortunately, Jesus' disciples deemed his time to be better spent on others—those with deeper needs and harsher woundings, those whose minds were better equipped for understanding.

Brevity and open displays of affection were not protocol for this Son of God. After all, he is a King. What would his royal subjects think? Better not to risk the displeasure of the courts. Better to keep the King removed from the reckless abandon of his children. Better to carefully guard the King's attachments—his fastenings and those fires he longs to kindle.

Jesus' response?

"Let the little children come to me."

Might he have been saying, "These little ones were meant for my attachment. They were meant for my lap. They are the means through which I will light a fire, the likes of which the world has never seen. They were meant for bread and wine and all things sacred. Let them come, and then let them come again. Do not hinder them. Let them receive my touch, for they know better how to receive the things of me and how to hold them in their hearts as sacred. Learn from them, ye men of protocol. They have painted for you a perfect picture of how one is to approach a King—without reserve and with the complete confidence of being received."

And so, not unlike our spiritual ancestors of Jesus' day, we broke protocol yesterday. We dared to risk a second helping of grace. In doing so, we remembered this one named Jesus and left our time together fuller for having been to the table.

When was the last time you approached your Father with such boldness and confidence? When has your pursuit of him led you to abandon the opinions of man in order to fasten yourself to his side? When did you last choose divine attachment over worldly strongholds? Today is the day to come to the table of grace and feast on the sustenance of a Father's love. He is looking for a few reckless children who dare to step beyond protocol and simply voice the desire for a second helping of everything Jesus.

His response to us?

> I am the bread of life. He who comes to me will never go hungry, and he who believes in me will never be thirsty.
>
> —John 6:35

Accordingly, as we run toward him for the "filling," sacrament with the Sacred is tasted, and our Father is well-pleased to kindle our hearts with the divine spark of his love. Communion is God's gift to us all; may we always be found with a childlike faith that isn't afraid to ask for more. Thus, I pray—

Father, you are the feast for my hungry soul. Thank you for allowing me to approach the table of grace with deep want and unsatisfied hunger. Thank you for your portion of love and relationship that far exceeds first and second helpings. I want more of you, Lord. More of your bread, more of your water, and more of the divine sustenance that fills the gnawing ache within my soul. Give me this day, my daily bread, and then, tomorrow, my daily bread, until one day I taste your bread face-to-face. Amen.

Peace at church

A further pause . . .

- What do you think stirs the heart of God most about a tender, childlike faith?

- How does a child's understanding about "who God is" sometimes speak a better witness than that of an adult's?

- How do religious practices sometimes hinder our bold and confident approach to God?

- Write the definition of "faith" according to Hebrews 11:1. How does this definition fit with a child's understanding?

a sacred doing

Hear, O Israel: The LORD our God, the LORD is one. Love the LORD your God with all your heart and with all your soul and with all your strength. These commandments that I give you today are to be upon your hearts. Impress them on your children. Talk about them when you sit at home and when you walk along the road, when you lie down and when you get up.

—Deuteronomy 6:4–7

Church is a family business around here. Doing life with Jesus isn't an option in our home. Hearts may refuse the deeper "doing"—the sacred work of the cross. But as it pertains to our physical "doing," to our comings and our goings and our stops between the two? Well, there is compliance on the part of my children, at least for the seasonal eighteen years beneath our roof.

It sounds harsh, legalistic, and intrusive, but as parents charged with the sacred trust of "training up a child" in the way of holiness, we understand that church serves as an ample shaping ground. At least it should. If church isn't your thing, if for some reason you've come to the conclusion that your church is doing more harm than good, then it is time to revisit the issue. Maybe even time to find a new church.

Why? Because church was never instituted for our harm. Church was given to us as a gift, as a celebration, as a way of gathering hearts in one accord for the unified worship of the one God who is worthy of our reverent pause.

It's not about programs and seeing how much we can cram into a worship service in hopes of raising our emotional fervor. It's not about worship preferences, a rocking band, a stoic tradition, or even the dressing of our flesh. It's not about who knows more, who seems less, who offers little, who tithes best. It has nothing to do with pageantry and pomp and circumstances created to boast a better faith than that of the competing churches down the road.

We may think it does, and in many ways, the best of these things often enhance our time of church participation, thus leading us closer to the heart of God. But to limit our church experience within such parameters—to define the quality of our faith based on these self-imposed guidelines—is to limit the sacred worth behind God's intention for our gatherings.

That worth is based on something far greater—a grander intention that cannot be matched by our feeble attempts at the same.

Peace at church

Church should be a place where we gather to know God. Any other intention falls subject to this overriding one. We may institute all manner of routes to get there, but at the end of the day, only one path leads us to the heart of the Father . . .

The cross of Jesus Christ.

Churches that are willing to follow along this path are not obsessed with the peripheral "rest of it." Instead, the people are simply content to gather together in order to more fully examine and more profoundly entreat the Lover of their souls. Where two or three come together in God's name, he promises his presence (Matthew 18:20).

And this is one of the primary reasons why church is family business in my home. I am counting on the probability that when our Sunday gatherings commence, there will be at least two or three others who have gathered with a similar intention. I want my children to be in the path of other believers, giving them the opportunity for the sacred intersection of their hearts with the heart of the living God, who knit them together in his likeness.

Does it always work out that way? Not always, but does that mean we should stop our efforts along those lines? Should we forego our corporate worship because it sometimes feels contrived and fake and so seemingly full of pretense? When God seems to prefer the hidden corners of our gatherings rather than a full-blown revelation of himself, do we pout out the doors in hasty retreat never to return?

Further still, do we allow our children their choices about their participation? Are we content to coddle their preferences above God's mandate for their sacred shaping? Where does our obedience lie?

Church will never perfectly practice our faith. Wherever flesh gathers, problems seem to follow. It is the tension of an earthly pilgrimage—this warring between selfish living and selfless surrender. Still and yet, it is our road to walk. It is our path of privileged participation. We can refuse it, or we can bend to it. Either way, the road requires our feet and the feet of those we hold dearest.

Better to give church the benefit of our many doubts and believe that somewhere in our "doing" of it, we will come across our Jesus. And whenever that happens, friends, the kingdom of God is opened up for the partaking therein.

I don't want to miss the kingdom feast. I yearn for the joy of its sacred celebration; it is a desire I hold for my family, a yearning I pray for you. Thus, I bow my head and offer this humble plea—

Show us, Father, the glory behind our obedience to "do" church. Meet us as we gather, and humble us with your presence. Forgive us when we think that you could do it better. We are a selfish and foolish people to put our needs ahead of your purpose. We want to know you, God; and then out of that knowing, we want to serve your people with the truth. Keep us to church; root us in faith, and then carry us along the path until our willing obedience finds us safely in your arms, fully home, and finally at rest. Amen.

Peace at church

A further pause . . .

- Describe your church and your experience with "doing church."

- What is your most compelling reason for being there? What is the most compelling reason you can think of for *not* being there?

- What do you see as your role in making "church" happen?

- If "knowing God more fully" and "where two or three are gathered" is the recipe for a successful church gathering, then describe how this was fulfilled in the following scriptures:

    Nehemiah 8:1–6

    Matthew 16:13–20

    Acts 2:36–41

    Acts 16:25–34

- Why is it critical that church be a family business?

 *come. tarry. go.*

"If you keep your feet from breaking the Sabbath and from doing as you please on my holy day, if you call the Sabbath a delight and the L<small>ORD</small>'s holy day honorable, and if you honor it by not going your own way and not doing as you please or speaking idle words, then you will find your joy in the L<small>ORD</small>, and I will cause you to ride on the heights of the land and to feast on the inheritance of your father Jacob." The mouth of the L<small>ORD</small> has spoken.

—Isaiah 58:13–14

The moment is as vivid to me today as it was when I was five. I leaned over to my mother and asked her to read the words that were beyond my articulation—three little words etched at the base of the stained-glass cross that adorned the front of our sanctuary.

"Come. Tarry. Go," she replied. "It means you come, you stay awhile, and then you leave."

I feel the warmth of her breath in this moment of recall. Those words and that cross have shadowed my steps ever since. I felt them profoundly today as I participated in a doing that I've been doing for my entire life. A doing that has carved me, etched me, and filled me with the significance of my sacred worth. A doing that sometimes requires faith over feeling, mind over matter, willingness over weariness.

Today, my feet pilgrimed to God's house for a Sabbath observance. Not because I felt like it; my feelings would have left me as I was—in bed and nursing a cough and sore throat that, perhaps, warranted my absence. No, this morning's arrival at my church had nothing to do with my flesh and everything to do with my feet's submission to a heart's obedience.

Today, I walked to Jesus intentionally and dressed in my best simply because he is worthy. Any other half-hearted attempt at honoring him would be just that—half-hearted and "less than" and a whole lot like the world's painting of a Sunday's worth. A worth that levels toward self-soothing and "doing as one pleases," rather than regarding the better necessity—that which leads a heart to worship.

And therein lies the seeding of my nearly four decades of faith.

What pleases me is doing what pleases God, and what pleases God is my honoring of him—my recognition of his relevant and extravagant grace and how far it has traveled on my behalf—to a cross where he willingly *came*, sacrificially *tarried*, and resolutely *departed* once love's redeeming work had walked its course.

His pause at Calvary means everything to me. The longer I walk with Jesus, the more I understand the depth of his gift. I didn't understand it at the age of five. I'm not sure I fully understand it now, but lingering in the shadow of the cross compels me to make the journey. Not because it needs my reverence, but rather because I need its reminder.

Peace at church

Thus, I *come* to the cross on Sundays. I *tarry* beneath its lavish grace that allows me my remembrance and that fuels my *going* forth in the week that lies ahead.

It's not overly profound, and to some it might seem rather perfunctory and packed with obligation. But when I consider what's been wrought on my behalf, how foolish would I be to act to the contrary? To choose my pleasing over God's pleasure? To walk as if my honor is worthy of more homage than his?

Doing life with Jesus has always been my privilege. It's been yours too. All too often, though, our gratitude walks in stark contrast to grace's dispensation. Instead of finding our footing at Christ's feet, we allow our flesh the wisdom to walk its own intelligence. The problem with fleshly wisdom is that it will always choose self over the sacred—"my pleasing" over God's.

And when a Sabbath day begins to look like every other day, when we refuse to give a moment's tarry to the One who tarried long and deliberately in our stead, then we not only have forsaken our first love, but also we have robbed ourselves of the rightful inheritance that is ours as children of the living God.

Jesus Christ.

He is our lasting and very great reward (Genesis 15:1). Spending time with him in intentional and deliberate worship is never wasted. It's life-giving and heart-changing and moves our faith into a deeper place of obedience and understanding. *Coming* to the cross and *tarrying* with our Father in his truth enables our *going*—our moving on and our moving out to spread the witness of his love. Without such pause, our lives breathe void of the power that comes from contemplative remembrance.

Today I remembered. I walked to God's house, alongside my family, and took time to hear my mother's words ringing in my ears, even as they did in my long ago and far away. They still sing true. They still whisper fresh. They still and will forever be the remembrance of grace that shadows my steps until I reach the throne of heaven and sit at my Father's feet for always.

Come. Tarry. Go.

A worthy obedience. A worthy reward. Thus, I pray—

Thank you, Father, for a Sabbath's pause that allows me your gracious remembrance. Forgive me when I deem "my pleasing" as more substantial than yours. You fuel my forever with the only truth that seeds everlasting. May my coming and my tarrying always reflect the deep grace that I have known, and may my going always reflect my attending therein. Thank you for the cross, for love's redeeming work, and for your Son's obedience to both. And thank you for parents who took me to church, who filled my heart with the witness of your love, and who spoke the truth of a stained-glass cross with every submitted step of their journeys. You graced me greatly when you gave me their arms. Amen.

A further pause . . .

- How does the phrase "Come. Tarry. Go." relate to your personal journey with Jesus?

- How does it fit in with the Great Commission as recorded in Matthew 28:16–20?

- In which pause of the cross—the coming, the tarrying, the going—do you find your struggle? Describe.

- What memory from your earlier years has profoundly shaped your view about "doing life" with Jesus?

Peace at church

 kingdom carriers

The kingdom of God is within you.

—Luke 17:21

Kingdom carriers. There are days when I don't fully appreciate the calling. Like yesterday.

I didn't want to go to church. I did want to go. But then I didn't. But then I actually did go because, well, church is what I do, despite my fleshly wants.

My "want to" for doing church shifted once I realized that yet another "thing" would be required of me upon entering its doors. In the fray and busyness of the preceding week, I forgot about my scheduled turn to teach during the children's church portion of the service—a portion that coincides with the morning message.

The thought of missing out on the nourishment and rest that accompanies my spirit with the hearing of God's Word sent my mood into a sudden and downward spiral. I didn't want the responsibility of feeding God's children. I wanted to be fed. Sharing my faith wasn't on the agenda. Rather, I wanted to sit with it in isolation and in quiet communion. Just me and God and the words of the preacher admonishing me with the truth of Scripture.

It was a quick descent into the pit of "poor me." But just as quickly as I arrived, another thought arrived, crowding its way onto the stage of my pity. Something about the "little children and the kingdom of heaven belonging to such as these" (Matthew 19:14). I briefly fought to "stuff it," to bury it beneath my annoyance, but kingdom reminders aren't the burying kind. They are meant to surface, especially when they've been freshly tilled within the soil of a heart.

My heart.

Prior to my Sunday morning arrival, I spent a portion of my Saturday evening perusing many "kingdom" scriptures. I eagerly took to the diversion. After all, I'm a kingdom talker. There is something regal and royal and divinely fascinating about this language. But for all of the ways I can nobly script God's kingdom, for all of the twists and turns of my poetic vernacular, none speaks more majestically than when my kingdom talking turns into kingdom walking.

Luke's gospel confirms such truth:

Once, having been asked by the Pharisees when the kingdom of God would come, Jesus replied, "The kingdom of God does not come with your careful observation, nor will people say, 'Here it is,' or 'There it is,' because the kingdom of God is within you."

—Luke 17:20–21

Am I walking God's kingdom, or am I simply trying to impress others with its language? Do I believe God's kingdom to be a literal housing within my flesh or simply a figurative and spiritually-speaking adornment attached to my feeble frame in hopes of prettying up my perimeter? Are the noble bloodlines of a King running within and throughout my veins, or does my blood bleed a temporal illegitimacy awaiting adoption?

Have I come to a place of deeper understanding—of fully receiving the truth of what I've been given as a believer in Jesus Christ? Have you? Have you come to some conclusions in the matter of God's kingdom and his bestowing of it upon you?

Our walk embodies our answer. Thus, the question.

Are we merely kingdom talkers, or are we walking it out? Are we approaching life with the perspective that our everyday occurrences with everyday people are better served by their coming into contact with the kingdom of God living within us?

If our answer is "yes," if, in fact, we believe that we are the keepers of God's light and the tenders of his sacred wick, then our lives should be more reverent, more intentional, and more aware of the sacred responsibility we've been allowed.

We are kingdom carriers—those entrusted with the keys accordingly (Matthew 16:19). Wherever we walk, we carry the unshakeable, trustworthy, regal, and royal throne of our God with us. We bring God's kingdom into the world via our flesh (2 Corinthians 6:16). And once we come to his conclusion on the matter of our noble endowment, our flesh becomes all the more eager to concede its will to the kingdom cause and to the little children and to the many others who so desperately need the intersection of God's throne with their fragile becoming.

We bring that intersection, friends. It is our privilege to do so. God has entrusted us with the responsibility. Therefore, our "wants" take a back seat to his. At least they should. Flesh and faith will always make for an odd mix; still and yet, they are the divine coupling that so often yields eternal results.

God has chosen to allow his kingdom to pulse within our fragile flesh. His is a kingdom not of the burying kind, but rather one made for the inheritance that comes with walking our sacred bloodlines. Whether we walk them with a ready heart or with a reluctant obedience, the kingdom of God was given to be given.

Carry him well. Carry him willingly. Carry him knowing that the kingdom he has seeded in you is one of everlasting worth and in need of your liberality in this coming season of influence. Thus, I pray—

Peace at church

Keep me from my isolation, God, from my thinking that your kingdom exists for me alone. Forgive me when I am selfish of its bestowing upon another, especially your children. Grow in me my understanding of what it means to be your kingdom carrier. Humbly, I surrender my flesh for the cause. Replace my little with your much, and seed my heart with a willingness to intersect humanity with the royalty and regality of your welcoming grace. I feel unfit to house your kingdom. Thank you for the cross that continues to call me worthy of such an honor. Amen.

Peace for the Journey

A further pause . . .

- What images or thoughts do you associate with the word "kingdom" in both the literal and the spiritual sense? Can you trace any similarities between the two?

- Read the following scriptures and record what they have to say about God's kingdom:

    Mark 10:14–15

    Luke 10:8–9

    Luke 22:24–30

    John 18:36–37

    Romans 14:17

    Hebrews 12:28

    James 2:5

- In what places or situations in your own journey do you find it most difficult to wear your kingdom conferment? Why might that be?

- Write out Luke 17:20–21 on an index card to signify the truth of your card-carrying membership in the kingdom of God.

8
Peace around the table with the ancients

When he was at the table with them, he took bread, gave thanks, broke it and began to give it to them. Then their eyes were opened and they recognized him, and he disappeared from their sight.
—Luke 24:30–31

lunching with the ancients

Now faith is being sure of what we hope for and certain of what we do not see. This is what the ancients were commended for.

—Hebrews 11:1–2

I ate with the ancients today.

Before anyone takes offense, you need to know that when I call them "ancient," I do so in the spirit of Hebrews 11:2. It is a labeling of respect, meaning an "elder; of age; the elder of two people; advanced in life; a senior."[10] And in the context of the scripture, an ancient is an elder bearing the witness of a life built on the solid foundation of faith.

It is a fitting tribute to my friends who wear this title—women seasoned with gray and with the wisdom of walking a long life with God. We are in our sixth year of "doing lunch" on Tuesdays. We began gathering upon my family's arrival to this community, and rarely have we missed a week in that time.

I seek them out wherever I go. I suppose it won't be long until others might consider me as one of their "ancients." It is a label I will humbly accept, for to be numbered alongside the ancients of my today and the ancients listed in Hebrews 11 is, indeed, an honorable tribute.

The pilgrims who gathered at the table this afternoon walk deeply. On the surface, we may seem a little shallow, for rare is the occasion void of our laughter. We do our fair share of discussing politics, current events, doctor's visits, and an offering up of ideas on how to fix the problems within our community and church. Mostly, I just listen to their thoughts, and I am glad to do so, for they have stored up a lifetime of wisdom worthy of my pause.

But underlying all of our chatter, there runs a sacred thread of a well-spun truth that anchors us all to the table and keeps us coming back every Tuesday for more: faith, and the certainty of things therein.

For all of the changes that come their way, there are a few things they would voice as certain. Things like:

- This life is full of pain.
- This life is full of joy.
- This life is but a breath.
- This life is not the end.
- This life is to be celebrated because . . .
- This life is a gift from God.

Peace around the table with the ancients

More than likely, we have all lived long enough to voice a few of these certainties as our own. It takes awhile to come to some conclusions in these matters. Our youthful immaturity and need for reasoned parameters often prohibit our clarity.

When pain is present, it is hard to reason the joy. When life fades to the certainty of death, it is difficult to see beyond the grave. And when celebration goes unnoticed—seemingly forgotten and pushed under because the urgent desperation blankets the party with wetness—well, life unwraps more like a tragedy rather than the sacred wrapping of a gracious God.

Indeed, it takes years of well-worn living to reach some conclusions in this matter called "faith." My ancients have lived those years.

Some years have authored sadness. Since we moved here, three of my friends have buried husbands. One of them has buried a son. All of us have walked to the grave on behalf of loved ones—friends, family, and one of our own Tuesday gatherers. Many have been escorted to the hospital because their bodies have betrayed them. Surgeries and procedures have been their portion. There are tears and remembrances aplenty that speak the witness of such sadness.

Some years have authored joy. Untold numbers of family marriages, babies, graduations, and birthdays have passed through their hands in our time together. There have been parties, vacations, family reunions, and most recently, a wedding between one of our ancients and her manly ancient. Indeed, they must collectively store enough memories to fill a scrapbook the size of heaven. There are pictures and newspaper clippings that speak the witness of these treasured milestones.

My ancients know about years and about the threading that weaves them together. They know God, and they are wild and wonderful and just on the other side of "crazy enough" to believe that he is the one who holds the needle that sews them ever closer to their eternal home.

They walk toward heaven, rather than in swift retreat. And if they harbor any fear in the matter, they keep it from me. Somehow, they realize that their faith, their hope, and their certainty about the season soon to arrive are needed commodities in a world that suffers from self-centeredness and short-sighted visioning. They have lived long enough to get over their bitterness, to live with the unanswerable, and to surrender their need for control.

They simply live by faith, not by sight. And they would all tell you that this is a really good way to live, considering that their temporal vision seems to be fading with the passage of time. They have caught the vision of their forever, and that, my friends, is reason enough to lunch with the ancients every Tuesday.

I need to see, and they need to color the sacred canvas of their witness while the brush is yet strong and the paint is still wet. Like the saints of Hebrews 11, theirs is a portrait worthy of the throne room of heaven. They surround my life with the witness of faith. I accept their influence over me with gratitude. I want the surety of my tomorrow to breathe with a similar measure of their faith—a firm belief that the "now" is but a dress rehearsal for the "next."

I think perhaps at the end of the day—at the end of this journey—our "next" just might resemble a Tuesday table, labeled with our names and fully prepared for our arrival.

Lunching with the ancients. A worthy pause. A sacred moment. An incredible foretaste of a gracious plenty that always seeds certain and that forever yields eternal. Thus, I pray—

Thank you, Father, for surrounding my life with the ancients on Tuesdays. They breathe the witness of faith unlike any other women in my life. You knew I needed them, Lord, and with gratitude I accept their influence over me. Script my heart with their certainty, hope, and faith in the truth of who you are. They are sure of their tomorrows. Let my life breathe with the same measure. And when we all finally reach our home with you in heaven, it surely would be nice to have a Tuesday table with our names on it. Please tell Maxine that we won't be long in coming. Amen.

Peace around the table with the ancients

A further pause . . .

- Who are the "ancients" in your life? What have they taught you about living?

- Take time to read Hebrews 11 and consider the "ancients" listed. Which person would you most like to share a table with in order to glean some further wisdom and deeper, godly understanding?

- Think of one "ancient" you could reach out to in this season of living. What are some practical ways you can connect with this person? Bring your relationship with him or her before the Lord and, in obedience, respond to God's prompting in the matter.

finding our voices

But in your hearts, set apart Christ as Lord. Always be prepared to give an answer to everyone who asks you to give the reason for the hope that you have. But do this with gentleness and respect, keeping a clear conscience so that those who speak maliciously against your good behavior in Christ may be ashamed of their slander.

—1 Peter 3:15–16

Words are a gift.

They come packaged in all manner of wrappings. Some costly; some cheap. Some dainty; some bold. Some with exacting precision; some with multiple layers. Some with care; some with little thought. Some tied with bows of blessing; some tied with ribbons of regret.

Regardless of the packaging, words are ours to give. Never are they meaningless. Never are they unimportant. Rather, they are the extravagant expression of a mind's thinking and a soul's seeding. They are the overflow of a heart's pause.

For out of the overflow of the heart the mouth speaks. The good man brings good things out of the good stored up in him, and the evil man brings evil things out of the evil stored up in him. But I tell you that men will have to give account on the day of judgment for every careless word they have spoken. For by your words you will be acquitted, and by your words you will be condemned.

—Matthew 12:34–37

That which is planted deep within will eventually spring to harvest—outwardly and on display for others to view. Whether for kingdom purpose or for hell's determined intention, words are the measure of our hearts.

Better speak them well, don't you think?

A few days ago, I unwrapped the gift of another's words. She spoke them softly and privately, punctuating the fact that they mattered so much to her. She is new to my life—a beautiful addition to my "ancients." As a transplant to our community, she has lived in quiet anonymity for the past few years, caring for the needs of her husband. A neighboring "ancient" invited her to Sunday school, and since then she has become a fixture around our Tuesday table, both at lunch and at evening Bible study.

She is a quiet calm amidst the crazy chatter and chaos that often dominates our Tuesday gatherings. Perhaps because of her newness. Perhaps because of her personality. Perhaps, simply, because our noise allows her little voice in the matter! Regardless of our din, she welcomes our presence in her life, and we are the better for having her in ours.

This past Sunday, I taught our senior adult Sunday school class. I love breaking the bread of God's Holy Word with them, and this occasion would prove the same. We spent some time in Acts 13, discussing the church's "sending out" of Paul and Barnabas on a missionary journey to Cyprus. We then talked about the responsibility of our church to do the same—to be a sending church that fully equips the saints for the missionary work entrusted to us as believers in Jesus Christ and as participants in the Great Commission.

I challenged them to consider whether or not we were meeting our responsibility along these lines as a corporate body and also as individuals. Had they found their voices in the matter as it pertained to the giving of a reason for the hope they hold in their hearts?

It was a difficult question, and an even more difficult asking. Not because they didn't understand its intent, but rather because there are some who, even though they've been doing life with Jesus for a long season, feel uncomfortable with such articulations.

Could it be that years don't always seed answers? That length of life doesn't always yield reasoned responses? That decades of church attendance don't necessarily harvest personal faith?

Perhaps. And while there are several in the class who could accurately and powerfully voice the reason for the hope they possess, I suspect there are many who find themselves at a loss for words when the world comes knocking. I understand the difficulty of such wrestling.

Grappling with the reasoning behind our faith yields a good growth—a stronger understanding and a deeper rooting to known truth. When we refuse our participation in the matter, our voices languish in isolation and confinement and seed very little towards kingdom purpose. Perhaps this is why my new friend's words were such a gift to me.

After class was finished and the crowd dispersed, she simply gave me a hug and whispered the overflow of her heart. "I'm still finding my voice, Elaine. It hasn't fully arrived, but I am working on it."

Carefully measured and bravely articulated, the words of this quiet "ancient" painted the portrait of a faith in process. Hers is a faith that teeters on the edge of a safer silence, daring her heart a dangerous participation beyond its borders. She is moving closer in her willingness to step into the ring in order to hammer out some answers for the hope she holds within.

Thirty years my senior, this woman is the woman I want to be. I want to be a pursuer of God. Someone who doesn't have all the answers, but someone who is willing to fight for them. Someone who wisely values the silence as preparation for the season to come. A season that moves beyond the quiet pulse of a routine existence in order to enter the fray of conversation in hopes that my voice—God's voice—will be heard above the noise and clamor of a worldly, diminishing hope.

I want my words to be God's gift to all people. Not wrapped with cheap intention or with careless thought, but rather wrapped in the boldness and beauty of the grace that resides within. A seasoned grace that always testifies on behalf of kingdom gain with eternal perspective in mind. Thus, I pray—

Make me like her, Father, my new friend who isn't afraid to step out of her routine in order to find her voice. Seed me with her willing determination, and keep me to the process of my articulation for the rest of my days. Give me the wisdom and grace to know when to speak your purpose and when to keep my silence. Never let my fear keep me from wrestling with the faith questions that deserve an answer. Let my voice sing pure and with the careful precision that leads others to do the same. Above all else, let my words walk in love and with the gracious grace that you have poured into my heart through the gift of your cross. Amen.

Peace around the table with the ancients

A further pause . . .

- How would you articulate the reason for the hope of Jesus Christ you have within? Write out a brief response, and consider any areas where you need further clarification.

- Read the following scriptures, recording what they have to say about the words of our mouths:

    1 Corinthians 2:11–16

    2 Corinthians 2:14–17

    Colossians 3:15–17

    2 Timothy 2:14–19

- Are you still finding your "voice" as it pertains to speaking your faith? What are some practical steps you can take to strengthen your witness?

a treasured storing

Do not be afraid, little flock, for your Father has chosen gladly to give you the kingdom. Sell your possessions and give to charity; make yourselves money belts which do not wear out, an unfailing treasure in heaven, where no thief comes near, nor moth destroys. For where your treasure is, there your heart will be also.

—Luke 12:32–34

I watched my ancient friend gather her gold. Old gold—forgotten and stowed away, weathered by years of neglect. Included in the collection were necklaces, earrings, and even some tooth fillings that once crowned her mouth with their golden hues of permanence.

Those treasures that once screamed their importance in her life were now being gathered as fodder for the latest craze—gold parties. Scrapping your gold for cash has become big business in homes across America. Gold is in; other types of "themed" parties are dying a quick death.

Why? Because gold parties line our pockets with cash rather than requiring them to be emptied. How quickly our "sought afters" and "must haves" have become the less desirables that we are willing to surrender for a quick payoff—for money to spend on the next trend that captures our fancy.

For my friend, it probably has less to do with the "next buy" and more to do with the conclusion she has reached after almost eight decades of living: "Stuff" is fleeting. Those things that scratch an itch toward temporal satisfaction mean precious little to a life that now walks closer to home—closer to the finish line and to the receiving of a glorious kingdom that is meant to satisfy eternally. Who needs jewelry when heaven awaits?

Who, indeed?!

Jesus speaks to the pull that exists between temporal wants and eternal fulfillment. He charges his followers with the "letting go" of the fleeting and with the "cloaking" of the lasting—an enduring purse filled with the unfailing, untouchable, and indestructible treasures that await our arrival in our final rest. Indeed, we may not be able to take "it" with us when we go, but we can be certain that "it" is waiting for us when we reach our final destination.

A better trade if you ask me.

Storing and making. The Greek transliterated word "poieo" carries with it the idea of producing; bringing about; making ready; preparing; shooting forth; and my personal favorite, "to be the author of, the cause."[11] Storing up eternal treasures transcends the world's penchant toward hoarding; it cannot be measured or calculated through tangible means.

Rather, filling our purses with the unfailing gain of heaven mirrors the process of writing a memoir—of authoring words. One sentence after another. One paragraph. One page. One chapter built upon the previous one, on and on until a book is finished, where its every word matters and is necessary for the completed end. The final work reveals the witness of a life lived and walked with an eternal perspective in mind.

This is how the "authoring" of an authentic journey reads. A lifetime worth of words and deeds and a thorough faith, scripted and banked for a kingdom end that will exceed our "sought afters" and "must haves." A kingdom, not lined with the paper and loose change of man's ambition, but rather with the bounty of an undeserved, yet rightful inheritance that is ours because of the Father's willingness to surrender his gold—his Son—to the purifying flames of a sanctifying grace.

We may not see the fullness of that inheritance in this day. Rarely do we feel it and, even less likely, do we ever understand it. We simply live in the certainty of it, knowing that our faith will soon be made sight. And when it is, when faith gives way to the glorious rewards of a long and mostly unseen obedience, we will witness the bounty of our deliberate storing. Only heaven is strong enough, deep enough, wide and completely vast enough to bank that kind of faith.

We may not "count it all a joy" now, but we will then, after we make one faithful choice after another, until we realize that every current, spirit-spoken "yes" in our hearts has reaped for us an eternal and resolute "yes" in our Father's.

> Well done, good and faithful servant! You have been faithful with a few things; I will put you in charge of many things. Come and share your master's happiness!
> —Matthew 25:21

Indeed, a better trade—one I am more than willing to scrap my gold for, because banking my treasure on anything other than Jesus Christ is a faulty and fleeting endeavor. Tangible wealth is an easily "tampered with" wealth, because tangible can be touched. The world is filled with willing pilferers and embezzlers who lie in wait to relieve us of our treasure.

But the Truth—the person, Jesus Christ, broken and poured out for the forgiveness of all sin? Well, he cannot be touched, for he is the eternal breath of heaven. He is the keeper of those who have lavishly spent their lives on his behalf and who have invested his love into the lives of others for kingdom's sake and kingdom's gain.

In the end, Jesus is the only "sought after" and "must have" who reaps eternal. Who loves eternal. Who spends eternal. Who rewards eternal. Who authors eternal. Thus, I pray—

Peace for the Journey

Write me in, Father, to your eternal manuscript that pens the eloquence of a life lived wholly and completely in accordance with your will. Fix my eyes on the unseen treasures of an abundant storing that happens now, on the front side of a final and certain witness that is soon-to-be. Thank you for the temporal treasures you have allowed in my life—treasures that bring comfort and joy and sustenance for this journey. Forgive me when they become too much, too important, and too necessary. You are my strength and my very great reward. How I look forward to sharing heaven with you. Amen.

A further pause . . .

- Consider the earthly treasures—your "must haves" and "sought afters"—that you currently store in your possession. Which of them could you easily surrender? Which ones don't seem as necessary as they once did?

- In what ways are you "storing up" some treasure for heaven? What are you "authoring" in this world that will be added to your kingdom account?

- What do the following scriptures have to teach us about "laying up treasure" for eternity?

    1 Timothy 6:17–19

    2 Corinthians 3:7–4:7

    Colossians 2:2–3

    Genesis 15:1

praying like ms. iris

This is the disciple who testifies to these things and who wrote them down. We know that his testimony is true. Jesus did many other things as well. If every one of them were written down, I suppose that even the whole world would not have room for the books that would be written.

—John 21:24–25

I listened to her pray today at our Tuesday lunch gathering. Her words voiced in unison with the apostle John's heart. Something along the lines of, "God, if we were to take the time to thank you for all of your goodness—for all of the ways that you've blessed our lives—we'd be here all day. Thank you for your many blessings and for allowing us some time around this table to be with one another. You have been so good to us."

Indeed, hers is a prayer that mirrors the sentiment belonging to the beloved disciple, John.

I love to hear Ms. Iris pray. Not because she's an expert in the "art" of praying, but rather because she's real when she does so. There's nothing fake flowing out from her heart. No hidden agenda. No "let's make a deal" before the throne. She's lived long enough and been through enough to shed the cloaking of pretense. Her eight decades of living have earned her the extraordinary privilege of knowing what is "good" and what is lacking.

Thus, when she thanks God for his goodness, you can take her at her word. She understands the fullness of what that means. She doesn't base God's goodness on her temporary set of circumstances. She recognizes that his goodness isn't conditional but, rather, is eternal—outlasting the ebb and flow of her day in, day out.

This doesn't mean she doesn't have some moments of pause—moments when her love for and confidence in God deepen into a fuller conversation that is peppered with an honest search for some unseen answers. Ms. Iris isn't afraid to ask the hard questions, to probe the depths of her faith with a sacred wrestling and to speak when others in her age bracket are often resigned to keeping silent. She doesn't bury her past. She carries it, deals with it, and is willing for others to partake of it if she thinks it might buoy them along in their journey towards truth.

I appreciate the gift of participation. In receiving her life into my own, I better understand what it is to grow in grace and to walk in rich thankfulness for the measure of time I've been given on this earth. And should I live to be eighty, should I be granted a few more years beyond this one, or even if this year is my last, I want to walk them all with a faith that prays like Ms. Iris . . .

Peace around the table with the ancients

Uncluttered. Unencumbered. Truthful, and to the point.
To do so, I must settle my heart and mind on a few abiding truths:

- God is good. Period. His inherent goodness is not based on my getting what I want. Long before my heart began pulsing, his heart was beating for me, was thinking about me, and was orchestrating my life into his very good plan.
- I don't need to know all of the answers. I simply need to rest in the confidence that he holds them and that one day soon, they will be mine to cradle for always. But until then, in this season of living that sometimes walks hard and contrary to my understanding . . .
- My God is okay with my conversations along these lines. He doesn't balk at my words, doesn't hide when my thoughts are not his, nor when my motives voice their partial understanding into the equation. God is wholly and completely familiar with all my ways because . . .
- My God created me and loves me with an everlasting love. Nothing I can say to him will change his opinion regarding my value. Why? Because . . .
- I was created in his image and my heart is seeded with a portion of eternity within. I was made for kingdom living, kingdom loving, and for walking in the way that leads me home to my Father.

Thus, God is good; he holds the answers, and he doesn't mind my asking for them because he loves me and has created me to be his kingdom companion on an everlasting journey. When we hold these truths as certain, our conversations with God will flow with all the natural ease and exposure intended for an intimate relationship between a Father and his child.

This is what I hear when Ms. Iris offers her voice to the God who created it. Her raw and unedited approach to life is laced with a timely and steady grace that has woven its portion of beauty into the fabric of all that she is and all that she does. Ms. Iris lives simply, but she loves abundantly. And she prays all the more.

May my heart and my life be so inclined to breathe the same.

Uncluttered. Unencumbered. Truthful, and to the point. Thus, I pray—

May the prayers of my heart, Father, be bold and unafraid to speak the penchant therein. May the truth of who you are always exceed my hesitation. Shower me with your acceptance, giving me room to breathe my thoughts before you without any condemnation or struggle from the enemy. You created me for intimate fellowship. May my life always reflect my desire for the same. Amen.

A further pause . . .

- Consider your prayers. How do you pray? Like Ms. Iris—unencumbered and with all the truth of your heart—or otherwise? Please describe.

- Of the five truths listed above, which one do you struggle with the most as it pertains to your understanding of God and your prayer life?

- Do you agree with the apostle John and Ms. Iris that, in fact, our God's goodness exceeds the parameters of what can be contained in print? Why or why not?

- Hear the truth of Scripture as recorded in Hebrews 1:3. "The Son is the radiance of God's glory and the exact representation of his being sustaining all things by his powerful word." Contemplate the goodness you have known through the hands of our sustaining God. Remind him of his goodness today by writing a prayer of thanksgiving, revisiting that goodness via your voice and your pen.

Peace around the table with the ancients

concluding exhortations

Let love of the brethren continue.

—Hebrews 13:1

Concluding exhortations.

That was the topic of this morning's senior-adult Sunday school class. I am not on the circuit of regular teachers for this group, but I have been attending their class for nearly three years. I dearly love them, both collectively and as individuals. Their words drip with wisdom, and their love breathes genuine. They've lived long enough to find their compass—to anchor their hearts within a centered peace and an abiding faith that are not easily shaken.

So when I was asked to offer my voice as their leader, I welcomed the opportunity. Hebrews 13:1–16 served as the backdrop for our discussion. It is a to-do list of sorts. Some final thoughts to punctuate the previous twelve chapters, detailing the supremacy and sufficiency of Jesus Christ. A list that includes:

- Loving one another.
- Entertaining strangers.
- Remembering those in prison.
- Keeping sexual purity at a premium.
- Keeping a love for money at a minimum.
- Finding contentment in the "have," realizing that the "have"—Jesus Christ—is all we'll ever need.
- Receiving the truth of that "have" as changeless—yesterday, today, and forever.
- Imitating the faith of the saints.
- Guarding the gospel as the truth.
- Bearing the reproach of Christ.
- Offering the praise of sacrifice.
- Doing good and sharing that goodness with others.

Indeed, some final, heavy thoughts packed into sixteen verses of Scripture duly categorized by modern-day translators as a few "concluding exhortations." And for all of the ways I could have taken the lesson this morning, sticking with the theme of this one phrase was the right way to go.

I asked the class members to consider their concluding exhortations. Exhortation, as found in Hebrews 13:22, is the Greek word "paraklesis," meaning, "The act of exhortation, encouragement, comfort. All of Scripture is actually a 'paraklesis,' an exhortation, admonition, or encouragement for the purpose of strengthening and establishing the believer in the faith."[12] Thus, I challenged my pupils, whose wisdom and maturity surpass mine by at least three decades, to pause and to consider what they might like to say as a concluding word of encouragement to a world that desperately needs the exhortation of such godly influence.

It is a tough question to ask, especially to souls who are aging and who, undoubtedly, live with some memories and pains and regrets that shadow them in these golden years of living. But tough is not always wrong, and this morning, tough was very right and became the tender soil of God's plowing. I witnessed my students' tears of understanding as we marshaled our way through sixteen verses of "forget-me-nots."

They laced the discussion with their laughter, their memories, their truth, and God's truth. And as quickly as the ten o'clock hour arrived, it left, and I was stunned by the provision of God's grace and presence that arrived on the scene to partake in our discussion.

His presence is his promise to us:

> Keep your lives free from the love of money and be content with what you have, because God has said, "Never will I leave you; never will I forsake you." So we say with confidence, "The Lord is my helper; I will not be afraid. What can man do to me?"
>
> —Hebrews 13:5–6

Indeed, if there is one exhortation that radiates from the hearts of the Friendship Sunday School Class, it is this simple truth. Throughout a lifetime of living, God has been faithful to live it with them.

Man has already done his doing over their lives—years' worth of doing that have left some scars. But the fear? Well, it is mostly gone now, for they have learned the secret of being content. In little and in much. In sorrow and in joy. In sickness and in health. In the present and in the tomorrow. Each day bears witness to the truth of an abiding Jesus, and they all have reached the conclusion that Jesus is, in fact, worth their living.

This is why they were there this morning, present and accounted for in a "doing" they've been doing for a long season. This is why I was there this morning and will continue to attend the senior-adult Sunday school class at my church. The class members live and breathe a "concluding exhortation" worthy of my pause—worthy of my embrace. They warrant my time and my preparation, for they are my brethren, and my love for them and theirs for me continues.

That love is deeper, stronger, and fuller with every conversation we share. We are a Hebrews 13:1 loving kind of people. We are working on the other verses, but this love thing, we are living it; and it is my great joy and privilege to be living it alongside of them. Thus, I pray—

Make me like them, Lord. Let my life breathe a concluding exhortation that includes love as its anchor. Keep me close to the wisdom of these saints, even closer to your truth, so that we may grow as one body in the unity and grace given to each one of us through your cross. Give me ears to listen, a heart to receive, and a hand to serve these precious friends of mine. Give them, each one, the strength to find their voices and the praise to find their lips so that their final chorus sings with a faith that will resound throughout the generations to come. Thank you for the privilege of their companionship along the road. They have been your grace to me, and I am the better for having them in my life. Amen.

A further pause . . .

- Read Hebrews 13, making careful note of the many "doings" required of God's people. In what ways are your "doings" doing well? Which "doings" could use some work?

- As a Christian, if you were to write a "concluding exhortation" to fellow pilgrims, what thoughts would you include?

- Hebrews 13:1 exhorts believers to "let love of the brethren continue." Why might the author of Hebrews begin God's "to do" list with the requirement of love?

Peace at home

Unless the LORD builds the house, its builders labor in vain.

—Psalm 127:1

a well-seeded heart

> *Whatever you do, work at it with all your heart, as working for the Lord, not for men, since you know that you will receive an inheritance from the Lord as a reward.*
> —Colossians 3:23–24

What do you do with a "doing" that is yours to do but that in truth you'd rather not do? Instead, you are content to let the "doing" slip from your fingers to do as it pleases, come what may. I know you know what I mean, but just in case you're confused, let me put it another way.

What do you do with your desires when they conflict with God's—when the task at hand doesn't match up with the "want to" that is residing within your will? I'll tell you what I do most days. I grunt and fuss and grumble my way through the doing, thus removing any fragments of a Jesus-light that was intended to shine through my willing obedience.

As a mother of four, the wife of a preacher, a leader involved in the life of the church, and a friend to many, my "doings" are often attached to the needs and desires of those who fill my world. Lately, they seem to have multiplied, thus wreaking havoc upon my will and intruding upon my personal desires. I imagine many of you could echo a similar refrain.

We are busy people, engaged with our "doing" at every turn. Somewhere between the task at hand and the completion therein lies the intentional walk of our wills. Our wills are shaped and molded by the fertile soil contained within our most extraordinary possession . . .

Our hearts.

The "doings" of our lives are fueled by the seeding of our hearts. What grows there grows outward and in abundance. And while our hearts are seeded with eternity (Ecclesiastes 3:11), unless cultivated under the Holy Spirit's guidance, our godly intentions easily can be replaced by another inclination so readily prevalent: evil. God said as much when he considered the hearts of his created people:

> The LORD saw how great man's wickedness on the earth had become, and that every inclination of the thoughts of his heart was only evil all the time.
> —Genesis 6:5

Peace at home

Jesus echoed the thoughts of his Father when he chronicled the heart's intent while instructing the Pharisaical dull and unenlightened:

> But the things that come out of the mouth come from the heart, and these make a man "unclean." For out of the heart come evil thoughts, murder, adultery, sexual immorality, theft, false testimony, slander. These are what make a man "unclean."
> —Matthew 15:18–20

So what do you do with a heart that is naturally predisposed toward evil?

It is a good question to ask and one that I've been pondering today as I have struggled in my doing for others. I confess that most of it has been fueled by a reluctant necessity rather than a willing "want to." Very little has been done as unto the Lord, and, quite frankly, I'm a bit weary of my "doings" no longer harboring the much-needed joy that should come from a well-seeded heart.

I'd like to suggest to you, according to God's Word, the solution—at least in part—for cultivating an "as unto the Lord" kind of heart. Doing our "doing" with a willing and ready obedience will never be our natural bent. Rather, it requires the cultivation of a three-step process. One step belongs to God. The other two belong to us.

God's step has already been accomplished. It exceeds the "how" of a plan to include a who—the Holy Spirit. "Because you are sons, God sent the Spirit of his Son into our hearts, the Spirit who calls out, 'Abba, Father'" (Galatians 4:6). Consider also, ". . . for it is God who works in you to will and to act according to his good purpose" (Philippians 2:13). A good heart is solely and completely based on God's Spirit living within a believing heart; accordingly, he fuels it with the capacity for a sacred and willing "doing."

The second step in the process of cultivating a willing heart is found in a story about sacred soil. "But the seed on good soil stands for those with a noble and good heart, who hear the word, retain it, and by persevering produce a crop" (Luke 8:15). A good and noble heart *hears* the Word, *retains* the Word, and *perseveres* in the Word until the harvest comes.

The third step of a divinely-seeded heart—a heart capable of doing all doings as unto the Lord—involves the intentional petitions of said heart.

> Do not be anxious about anything, but in everything, by prayer and petition, with thanksgiving, present your requests to God. And the peace of God, which transcends all understanding, will guard your hearts and your minds in Christ Jesus.
> —Philippians 4:6–7

A good heart prays about everything. In return, God promises to protect the heart with his careful and watchful guard.

So what's a heart to do with its "doing" when its nature is predisposed towards evil?

Acknowledge the power of God's Spirit living within you to cultivate a willingness for the "doing." Become a student of God's Word through the hearing of it, retaining of it, and the persevering in it until the grunt and grumble of your "doing" transforms into a ready willingness. Pray about everything, thus securing your heart's protection.

It's not an exhaustive list, but it's manageable. In fact, it is doable for those who are intent on doing all things well and with an "as-unto-the-Lord" kind of heart at the helm.

So, let's get to it. One verse at a time, one prayer at a time, one stubborn perseverance at a time, all under the watchful and careful guidance of God's Spirit within, until our "doing" feels more like a sacred privilege rather than a reluctant necessity. Thus, I pray—

Help us, Father, to do our life's work with your joy seeded deep within our hearts. Tend to our hearts through the power of your Holy Spirit, and grow in us the understanding that our lives are to be lived in grateful thanks and in a posture of willing doing "as unto the Lord." Forgive us for our grunting and grumbling, for we are the recipients of your sacred bestowing. Keep us mindful. Keep us surrendered. Amen.

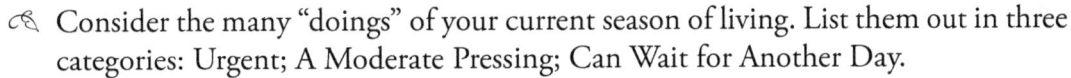

A further pause . . .

- Consider the many "doings" of your current season of living. List them out in three categories: Urgent; A Moderate Pressing; Can Wait for Another Day.

- As you peruse your list, which of your "doings" were done with an "as unto the Lord" kind of heart? Which were not? Consider the reasons for the disparity.

- Why do you think it is so easy for us to find our grunt and our grumble instead of our willingness when it comes to our many "doings"?

- Read the following scriptures to record what they say about the heart:

    Jeremiah 17:9

    Matthew 12:34

    Matthew 15:18

    Romans 2:29

    Romans 5:5

    2 Corinthians 1:22

    Colossians 3:1

    1 Peter 3:15

a golden moment

For unto us a child is born, to us a son is given, and the government will be on his shoulders. And he will be called Wonderful Counselor, Mighty God, Everlasting Father, Prince of Peace.
—Isaiah 9:6

I had one of those rare moments yesterday. A moment that spins golden and breathes pure. A moment easily missed if eyes and minds are focused elsewhere. Fortunately, my eyes and heart were open for the whispers of a better focus—a baby girl, asleep on the couch.

She really isn't a baby anymore. She is six years old, but as my only "pink" in line behind three "blues," she will always hold the title as my baby.

Rarely does she sleep during the day. She's outgrown such habits, but yesterday's quiet and the drone of the television lulled her into a late afternoon nap. Everyone else was somewhere else, and I was busy at the computer. When I hadn't heard from her in a while, I went into the living room and found her curled up on the couch. Instead of rousing her from her slumber, I gently picked up her frame and cradled her on my lap.

She barely noticed and continued with her ruffled breathing for the better part of an hour. I simply listened and held and prayed and cried some tender tears for the moment. It won't be long before my cradling of her tiny body will be beyond my reach. Literally. But her heart? Always within reach. Always fit for my cradling, my holding, my praying, and my tears of celebratory and unwavering love.

She is a gift to me. I never imagined her. As a single mother of two young sons, I never imagined much beyond my survival. But then my husband, Billy, and then the gift of a third son. And then a friend who jogged by my house one afternoon, proclaiming to me that God had strongly spoken a word into her spirit about my having another child. I laughed and said "thank you." Sort of.

I wasn't planning on another child. But then one November day, I began to notice a shift in my body. Something was going on. Baby girl was going on, and now, six years down the road, I am the better for plans gone awry. God interrupted my life with Amelia, and my heart, already so full to the brim with love for my family, ripped open once again to receive the gift of a daughter.

She's growing so fast, so good and so full of fresh perspective. I see her take to her Jesus, even as I took to him at her young age. She goes beyond the Christian talk. She's walking her Christian talk. And last night, as a witness to the stirrings of her heart, she made a picture for me. It reads, "I love Jesus. Jesus is the star. Jesus is the best! He rocks. He is the baby. He is the son of God."

In her tiny, fragile, six-year-old way of understanding, my daughter weaves a pretty stable theology. Her words are simple. Her faith is growing. And her heart remains, for the most part, untainted by the world's insistence to the contrary. There will come a day for hurts—for her questions and for some unbelief. But right now, Jesus rocks. He's the best thing she's got going on, and she isn't afraid to allow him some praise via her pen.

She's teaching me to do the same. It's not always easy to be taught "faith" through the simplicity of a child. But I think, perhaps, our propensity towards making faith a difficult road could use a swift and prolonged detour to a couch and to the whispers of a younger season, when innocence ruled the day.

Our lives are too crowded. We are concerned about a great many things while neglecting the tender pull of our heart strings. We long for life to sing its beauty, but rarely are we willing to pause for a listen. Beauty has never been absent. She has always been singing her song. But us? We have perfected our absence. We choose it every time we choose . . .

- busy over the best;
- chaos over the calm;
- computers over the couches;
- schedules over the sacred.

We miss the loveliness of a moment because moments can sometimes breathe so singular—so set apart and so seemingly unnecessary as it pertains to the whole.

Shame on us for not thinking that a single moment can change everything.

Single moments are the stuff of eternity. Single moments shape and sharpen and hone a heart for hugeness. Single moments breathe with the promise of a grander epic. Single moments collect and gather to form a destiny that exceeds the temporal and the seen.

I had one such moment yesterday. A single pause that spun golden. I held a child in my arms and knew that my life has been and will always be better because of the holding.

Over two thousand years ago, there came a moment that spun golden for another mother and her child. Months earlier, a friend of sorts stopped by her house and spoke a word of witness into her spirit.

> But the angel said to her, "Do not be afraid, Mary, you have found favor with God. You will be with child and give birth to a son, and you are to give him the name Jesus. He will be great and will be called the Son of the Most High. The Lord God will give him the throne of his father David, and he will reign over the house of Jacob forever; his kingdom will never end."
>
> —Luke 1:30–33

A single moment. The stuff of eternity, and we are all the better for the holding of the child.

We relive that golden moment every year in December. It is a stabled moment that is worthy of consideration year-round in order for us to glimpse God's best. To witness the Son who has rocked our worlds with his arrival into our hearts. To give our Star the stage that he deserves and to applaud his performance with our hearty "hallelujahs" and grateful "amens."

His name is Jesus, and he's never too old for our cradling, our holding, our prayers, and our tears of celebratory and unwavering love. May your couch and your deliberate pause therein capture the glimpse of God's best in this season and for always. Thus, I pray—

Oh come, oh come, Emmanuel, and ransom us from our captivity with the truth of your grace. Keep us mindful of your shining moments and weave them into our own. You are the only Star worthy of prominence and adoration. When our busyness becomes too burdensome, when our current remains too crowded, bring us to the couch for sacred pause—for remembrance and for the renewal of your profound truth that reads with the simple faith of a child. May your rest be our portion this day. Amen.

Peace at home

A further pause . . .

- Describe a time in recent history when you "paused" long enough to breathe in the truth of Jesus.

- Examine the "crowding" in your life that keeps you from experiencing these moments on a consistent basis. What are some practical steps you can take to minimize your "crowding" in order to maximize your sacred moments?

- Take time to read Gabriel's announcement to Mary in Luke 1:26–38. Consider the day when you first received the good news of Jesus Christ. In what ways does your experience mirror hers?

brotherly love

Therefore I stationed some of the people behind the lowest points of the wall at the exposed places, posting them by families, with their swords, spears and bows. After I looked things over, I stood up and said to the nobles, the officials and the rest of the people, "Don't be afraid of them. Remember the LORD, who is great and awesome, and fight for your brothers, your sons and your daughters, your wives and your homes."

—Nehemiah 4:13–14

Some things are worth fighting for. Some people, all the more. Just ask my son.

While driving the carpool Friday afternoon, I listened to my eight-year-old explain to his sister and her friend his strategy for playground defense should the need ever arise. It went something like this: "If they won't leave you alone on the playground, here's what you do. First, you could tell the teacher. Or, you could just ignore them. Or, you could walk away. Or, if that doesn't work, you could just find me."

He was very serious, and I was amused. At least in part. My other part was internally screaming my motherly "hoorahs" for a son who loves his sister; so much so, that he is willing to protect her from the wild and wooly of a playground taunt.

I never knew the protection of an older sibling's love, so when I witness it between my own children, I am drawn to the magic of their deep bonding. And while they occasionally rival their passions and wills with all the fury of Pamplona's running of the bulls, their love for one another always exceeds their momentary sparring.

As it should.

Family love roots deeply, and if those with whom we share our homes cannot be trusted to love us, and, therefore, protect us whenever the taunts of the playground mock their insistence, we are left to our solitary efforts at defense. And as defense goes, two are always better than one, especially when one of the two is bigger, stronger, and solely motivated by the sacred trust of family bloodlines.

The prophet Nehemiah understood the value of familial love. He exposed its depth by instructing the Israelites to work in families while repairing the walls of their beloved homeland. He understood that corporate focus would yield greater results than individual determination. The taunters of their playground were very real and very likely to make good on their threats. Single determination wouldn't be enough to build the second half of Jerusalem's walls. It would take the family—God's family—working on behalf of one another and on behalf of a cause they deemed worthy of the potential peril involved.

That cause?

The kingdom of God.

"Remember the LORD, who is great and awesome, and fight for your brothers, your sons and your daughters, your wives and your homes" (Nehemiah 4:14). Not, "Fight hard because if you don't, you and your family will die." Not, "Fight because you have no other options." But rather, fight because you've got a God worth fighting *for*—a great and awesome God who is worthy of your walls and your best efforts at protection.

When the Israelites forged ahead in their rebuilding with a hammer in one hand and a sword in the other, they did so knowing that they were fighting *for* something rather than against something. They were fighting *for* the preservation of God's kingdom and *for* the rightful place of their families within it.

When the playground warfare surfaced, there was no telling the teacher or ignoring the taunts of their enemies. There was no option of simply walking away from the threats. For walls to be built, there had to be laborers willing to put their hands and their hearts to the task. Thus, the option remaining for their playground defense—according to an eight-year-old and according to the prophet Nehemiah—was to find a bigger brother, a bigger sister, or a bigger family that was completely and "holy" motivated by the sacred trust of family bloodlines. And motivated by a love that roots *for* the life-giving truth that there is a great and awesome God worth preserving and that he is the only worthy gain of our hearts in the end.

Walls will come and go, friends. But God? Well, he remains. And if we're not willing to fight *for* the truth of who he *is* so that our brothers and sisters, our children and our parents, our neighbors and our friends might live and walk in that truth, then we are forsaking the sacred trust of our family bloodlines. When we are no longer willing to put our lives on the line *for* the sake of our families' salvation, then we have limited the grace of the cross, which was never ours to constrain.

We are tied to Emmanuel's veins. They bled long and wide and high and deep so that you and I can find our rightful place in the kingdom that is now, that is to come, and that is solely within our Savior's right to give.

When the truth of Calvary becomes the taunt of the playground, telling the teacher, ignoring the threats, or walking away seeds very little toward kingdom gain. But walking the perimeters of the playground with familial love as your anchor? Well, this is when walls find their framing, families find their strength, and the enemy finds his eventual retreat.

Peace for the Journey

Indeed, some things are worth fighting *for*. Some people too. One God, all the more. And in case you're still not convinced, just find my son. He's got a few things to say in the matter and the faith to back it up. Thus, I pray—

Keep us to our walk of faith, Father, both at home and on the playground. Let us not fear the taunts of the enemy, but let us stand firm in the truth of your love for us. You are building us into your everlasting kingdom, where the stones of our lives come alongside one another to build a beautiful witness of your promise and grace. Let us not forsake our voices and our hands in the process. Keep us to our mortar and to your sword until the wall is finished and our family—your family—is safely within its shelter. Amen.

A further pause . . .

- Consider a time when you had to fight on behalf of someone you love. What motivated your involvement? What stood to be lost had you not intervened? What was gained in the end?

- What are some issues facing your family that you are willing to fight *for* on a regular basis?

- What are some of the issues facing the body of Christ that force your participation?

- What guidelines do you use to gauge your participation? How do you choose when to get involved and when to remain on the sidelines?

- Take time to read about the opposition that the Israelites faced while rebuilding Jerusalem's walls as found in Nehemiah 4. Describe the tactics of the enemy. List the tactics that the Israelites employed in facing the enemy.

benedictions

Now may the Lord of peace himself give you peace at all times and in every way. The Lord be with all of you.

—2 Thessalonians 3:16

The call came in just a few minutes ago—7:48 AM, per usual. Normally, I catch the call, but the phone was hiding elsewhere this morning. There was nothing new about his message. It was just his voice reminding me that he had safely made it to his destination . . . "Hey, Mom. I'm here at school. Have a good day. Love you. Bye."

His words interrupted my train of thought—a train hunkered down in the middle of 2 Timothy and the apostle Paul's chains. I looked up for a moment and tearfully echoed my response to my son with an outstretched hand extended in the direction of the answering machine . . . "Love you too, baby. Go with God today. Be with God. Let him be your light."

He couldn't hear me. But God could; and between the two of us—God and me—a message of peaceful intention was instantly carried from this mother's heart to the heart of her child, despite the ten-mile chasm between us.

With those few words of exchange, albeit spoken into the air and without the benefit of face-to-face communication, my thoughts have shifted from Paul's chains toward, the pondering of something else.

Paul's benedictions.

From Romans to Hebrews, and in every book in between, Paul concludes his teaching letters with a benediction—words of blessing and final encouragement. Words such as:

Now to him who is able to establish you by my gospel and the proclamation of Jesus Christ . . . to the only wise God be glory forever through Jesus Christ! Amen.

—Romans 16:25–27

The grace of the Lord Jesus be with you. My love to all of you in Christ Jesus. Amen.

—1 Corinthians 16:23–24

May the grace of the Lord Jesus Christ, and the love of God, and the fellowship of the Holy Spirit be with you all.

—2 Corinthians 13:14

Peace at home

Words like that. And even though the recipients of said words, both then and now, didn't hear them as I imagine Paul voicing them while he penned them, God did. God does. And between the two of them—the Holy Spirit and Paul—a message of peaceful intention has been carried from one saint's heart to another, despite the two-thousand-year chasm between us.

Paul understood the power of a blessed benediction. He punctuated his "hard" teachings with words like "grace" and "peace" and "love." And while we may not fully understand the depth of all that Paul was trying to say within his letters, it is easy for us to receive and to get our hearts around his endings.

As it was with Paul's "sincerely" and postscripts, so it is with ours. Thus, a question or two.

How goes it with the blessed ending of our words? The crescendo of our communications? The climax of our conclusions? The closing of our conversations?

How do we punctuate our exchanges with humanity? When others walk away from our wordy embraces, do they walk away with grace and peace and love? Or do they walk away with something to the contrary? With confusion, sorrow, bitterness, nothingness?

When we close our letters, when we finish our phone calls, after we spell-check our e-mails and polish our correspondence into ship-shape, when we conclude our meetings in the board room or around the kitchen table, when we finally reach the end of all that we're trying to say, how will we say it? Furthermore, will we say it, or will we leave our words dangling in mid-air, hoping for their soft landing and subsequent understanding but not giving much thought to their conclusion?

Benedictions. They are ours to give, ours to write, and ours to speak. When we refuse them their voice, we've spoken less, even though God intends for us to speak more. His more—his words when we've finally come to the end of ours.

It's not all about the preacher's moment. We think it is. After all, benediction is a bulletin word—a "holy" kind of word that follows the sermon. But you and I, we are a holy kind of people who are bringing God's truth to this world. Our lives are intended to read as a sermon. And when we get to the end, a little grace and peace and love is the perfect punctuation to a well-spoken and well-lived life.

I don't want my words or my life to conclude with confusion and nothingness. I want my benedictions to read everlasting and on purpose so that years from now they will serve as an enduring memorial from my heart to the generation of hearts who are coming up behind me. They may not hear my words now, even as I voice them while I type, but between the two of us—my extraordinary God and me—I believe in their preservation.

May they always be found worthy of such sacred perpetuation. Thus, I pray—

Benedict my life with your sacred punctuation, Father, with your words of grace and peace and love. May the utterings of this mouth and the overflow of this heart be used to point others to the cross. Never let my busyness keep me from blessing others. Instead, remind me to finish well—my conversations and my life. Let the conclusion of my words be filled with the conclusion of your truth, and let your truth be the grand conclusion of the conversation that I now carry in my heart. Amen and amen.

A further pause . . .

- Consider your benedictions. Do you have a particular way you finish your conversations with others, either in person or in print? Describe.

- What might be some of the benefits of ending your conversations with a positive, defined punctuation?

- Take time to review some of Paul's benedictions that are included with his letters to the New Testament churches by writing them below:

    Galatians 6:18

    Ephesians 6:23–24

    2 Timothy 4:22

    Hebrews 13:20–21

- Modeling your thoughts after Paul's, write out your own words of benediction over someone you love. Practice speaking these words over him or her in the days to come.

where the heart is

For where your treasure is, there your heart will be also.

—Luke 12:34

I sensed my son's immediate discomfort with the statement spoken to him by a local parishioner while waiting in the check-out line at Wal-Mart®.

"Sure bet you're glad to be back home."

Nicholas squirmed, looking for a gracious response. "Yes, sir. It's good to be home."

Even as he spoke it, I felt the painful cut that seared his heart with more clarified precision than a sharpened knife. The words weren't intended to hurt, but they did. They reminded my son of everything he's been trying to process since returning home from Bolivia.

If home is where the heart is, then my son's home—at least for the "right now"—resides somewhere in the remote mountainous village of Tacachia, Bolivia. He spent the better part of a week walking its soil and tending to its harvest—a harvest that exceeded the fruit of the land to include the fruit of relationships.

The Kory Wawanaka Children's Home, an orphanage sustained through the Methodist Church of Bolivia, houses nineteen orphaned children, ranging in ages from three to thirteen. When Nick first visited their community last year, the orphanage had four residents. Newly licensed for operation, the home has experienced strong growth in every way during the past twelve months.

It was especially meaningful for Nick to witness the growth of the past year. The "pulse" behind the work there is strong and evident, stirring his heart for further involvement.

"I want to go back, Mom, and not just for a week. I want to stay longer next time."

Next time.

My heart can barely get around these past "two times." Still and yet, I listened to him pour his heart out over cheeseburgers and fries during a mother and son outing. I knew it was coming, this unwrapping of his feelings. Even as his emotions welled with the "telling," mine welled with the listening.

God is moving Nick's heart in a new direction. The shaping that's taking place is what I've prayed for his entire life. In fact, I've prayed this prayer for all of my children over the years—that they would, each one, know early on in their lives what God would have for them. That they would walk in their "callings" in their twenties rather than waiting until their forties to figure

Peace at home

it all out. That they wouldn't spend their days wondering about what they were supposed to be doing but rather would spend them knowing that whatever they were doing, they were doing so with an eternal purpose in mind. A kingdom purpose.

I prayed that they would find God, sense God, believe God, and know God in the everyday and mundane events of a life that doesn't always make sense but that is content to walk hand in hand with the One who possesses perfect sense and understanding for the road ahead. That they would listen to the promptings of God's Spirit within and not brush it off as a momentary whim or selfish fancy. That they would, in fact, trust in the truth they've been given as children of the Most High God. A truth that tells them God is living and active and moving on their behalf and that, because of this "constant working," they shouldn't be surprised when he shows up on the scene of their lives, prompting them to keep in step with his leading.

God is faithfully answering this prayer for Nick. I heard it in his words and saw it in his eyes as we shared a table and bared our hearts to one another. And while Nick has always imagined his life to be headed in a certain direction, God is daring him to imagine bigger. To dream better. To see beyond his raw capabilities and instead, to take hold of his sacredly-bestowed giftings.

This kind of living, friends, is where it's at. God has planted his own seeds of promise within our lives. When we begin to see those seeds harvested for kingdom gain, then our hearts, like my son's, welcome the growth of a fertile soil. In fact, our souls can't help but cry out for it, for the untilled lands of an untouched country that is completely and "holy" surrendered to the truth of God's unlimited possibilities.

As we connect with this kind of "heart-stirring"—when we begin to see our lives framed within the context of a greater good rather than within the parameters we've so carefully and comfortably created for ourselves—then we walk our part in the Great Commission. We walk our callings—no matter the location, no matter our age, no matter if we yet possess the credentials or the education to go alongside. We simply and profoundly walk our faith with all the confidence of heaven as our guide. We don't worry about the particulars. The details belong to God. But the steps? Well, they are ours to journey, whether here or abroad. When walked with the Creator, every step moves us closer to him—to heaven—where the final proclamation of our earthly life will resound in perfect unison with perfect wisdom.

"Yes, Sir, it's good to be home."

Home. The place where our lives were always intended to land.

By the grace of God, I'll get there. By his grace, so will Nick; so will my other children. So will you. Thus, I pray—

Peace for the Journey

Thank you, Father, for meeting us in this day. For showing up on foreign soil to till our hearts for kingdom purpose. For allowing us the "wrestling" with some things that further shape our understanding about how you intend for us to live. Give us the courage to "work the thing out" before you, with you, depending on you, so that we come to a greater place of obedience to you. Use our pain to teach us, Father, even when it hurts and our preferences call out for its burial. Meet us in those deep places; stir us all the more, and keep us to the pilgrimage of a final grace that will walk us home and welcome us fully. Amen.

Peace at home

A further pause . . .

- Describe a time when you've experienced a "heart-stirring" from God—a time when you knew that God was daring you to dream bigger and beyond your current situation. What set this experience apart from other moments of clarity you've had along the way?

- What was your response to God's nudging? Did you ignore it or tend to it?

- What might be the ramifications of ignoring God's promptings in your heart?

- Take time to read about Paul's "heart-stirring" moment as found in Acts 9:1–31. What was God's commission for Paul in verses 15–16? What was Paul's response, and how did his response benefit the cause of Christ in verses 19–31?

- How different would our spiritual history read had Paul not tended to God's calling upon his life?

- Spend some time in prayer, laying out your heart before God and asking him to clarify his dreams for your life; record your thoughts and commit them to his safe-keeping.

10
Peace on the road

They were talking with each other about everything that had happened. As they talked and discussed these things with each other, Jesus himself came up and walked along with them.
—Luke 24:14–15

Peace for the Journey

 on the road with Jesus

> *When he heard that it was Jesus of Nazareth, he began to shout, "Jesus, Son of David, have mercy on me!" Many rebuked him and told him to be quiet, but he shouted all the more, "Son of David, have mercy on me!" Jesus stopped and said, "Call him." So they called to the blind man, "Cheer up! On your feet! He's calling you."*
>
> —Mark 10:47–49

Jesus lived his earthly life in forward motion.

He was always on the go, on the road, in the know, and in the mood to be the person God intended for him to be. He came to do his Father's will. Never once did he forsake that will for the sake of his own will—some time off to depart from the "pressing in" of his pressing purpose. Even in his times of sacred pause, Jesus was still available and set on "go" for whatever or whomever God placed in his path.

Two thousand years ago, that "who" was a blind man named Bartimaeus. Jesus was traveling the road from Jericho when shouts for his divine favor reached his ears. Others tried to quell the neediness with their selfish approach to doing life with Jesus, but Jesus trumped their objections with his own agenda. It was an agenda that favored the needs of the one over the preferences of the many.

"Call him."

They did, and with their summons, Bartimaeus stripped off his outer covering and came boldly, blindly, and in his barren estate before the only one who was willing to tend to his cries. In the end, he received more than his longed-for sight; he received a healing that extended to his heart, which resulted in his following after Jesus "along the road."

Jesus was and continues to be a road Savior—a traveling God with a forward purpose in mind. We are that purpose. He never fails in his following after us, even when we fail to notice his pursuit. He simply and profoundly *is* wherever we are. Why?

Because we are what he came to do. We are the driving force behind his deliberate steps and his once-for-all sacrifice that propelled him forward to a cross rather than assigned him a place in anonymity. He chose the road of high and holy suffering because he knew we would be prone to walking our roads without the hope and belief that we were meant for anything beyond our current condition.

And for most of us, our current condition involves some suffering. If not in the flesh, then in the emotional and spiritual aspects of a pilgrimage grounded in a theology cloaked with the sacred tenet of a crucified life.

Peace on the road

> I have been crucified with Christ and I no longer live, but Christ lives in me. The life I live in the body, I live by faith in the Son of God, who loved me and gave himself for me.
> —Galatians 2:20

To live as Jesus lived, to walk as Jesus walked, is to embrace the road he paved with the blood-bought sacrifice of Calvary. It means that we can no longer walk in isolation from the pleas of the many. It means that we stop and bow low to wash some feet when our preference is to remain upright, preserved, and untouched by the unclean. It means that our "need to be heard" takes a back seat to the shouts of those who need it more. It means that we share Jesus with everyone, even when we prefer to keep him to ourselves.

Being on the road with Jesus, means exactly that. Being on the road. With Jesus.

Thus, we get to the road. We choose the dirt and dust of the street and do so knowing that we walk it with the road Savior, who always has his forward intention in mind. We cannot put parameters on the pauses he orchestrates along the way; instead, we must be willing to pause with him, to offer our voices and our touch accordingly, and to say with all the confidence and grace of heaven to those in need, "Cheer up! On your feet! Jesus is calling you!"

This is what it means to live our earthly lives in forward motion as Jesus did. When we grasp that, when we fully and completely realize that our "cheer" and our "pilgrim's progress" is directly linked to the fact that Jesus is calling us through purposeful intention, then we, like Bartimeaus, should throw all considerations to the side. We should sprint to our Savior's feet and offer him the one heart's plea that has the capacity to alter our forever . . .

"Rabbi, I want to see."

I don't know about you, friends, but I want to see because my Savior has enabled me to do so. I want to be a road warrior with Jesus—to walk where he walks, to stop where he stops, and to embrace those whom he embraces. Not because it is payment in part for the healing I have known, but rather because it is my privilege to participate with him on the way, along the way, and in the way of the crucified life.

I am not my own. I was bought with a price. I've been given a kingdom, and I want to spend the rest of my earthly days walking my royalty in step with my King. Thus, I pray—

Keep me to the path of a consecrated walk, Father. Lead me in your steps of understanding and with a breadth of wisdom that exceeds my own. Show me how to live my life in forward motion and to see with your eyes of grace rather than with the limited vision that so often strangles my faith. I surrender my feet to the road. I surrender my heart to yours. Make me your road warrior for life. Amen.

A further pause . . .

- Consider some familiar "stops" that Jesus made during his earthly pilgrimage. Describe.

- How do those "stops" fit with the description that Jesus is a "road Savior"?

- Please read the full account of Bartimaeus's encounter with Jesus as found in Mark 10:46–52. What did Jesus ask of Bartimaeus in verse 51? How did Bartimaeus respond?

- Describe a time when you called out for Jesus and he stopped to ask of you, "What do you want me to do for you?" What was your response to his question? How did God answer?

- Write out Philippians 4:19 on an index card and receive it as God's promise over your every need this day.

Peace on the road

love tied to a tree

This is how God showed his love among us: He sent his one and only Son into the world that we might live through him. This is love: not that we loved God, but that he loved us and sent his Son as an atoning sacrifice for our sins.

—1 John 4:9–10

I would have missed it if I had done what I wanted to do.

What I wanted to do was to sleep. What I did, instead, was to put on my running shoes and head outdoors for a little bit of routine and a whole lot of boring. While lacing up my shoes, I told the Lord this was a choice of my will, not of my "want to." He was going to have to push me out the door and get my feet moving. He agreed with my assessment. Thus, he pushed, and before long, my "want to" caught up with my will as I found my stride along my usual path.

The weather was cool and crisp, reminding me that winter's end has not yet come. The sun's brilliancy reminded me that spring's blossom is just around the bend. With headphones blaring and the pavement beneath my feet, I quickly found my rhythm, believing that the benefits of such an obedience would outweigh the boring. Benefits that include better health, better mind, and better spirit.

God has always used my time outdoors to accomplish this three-fold blessing. I allow him to teach me in these moments. I open up my eyes to see, my ears to hear, and my mind to conceive the possibilities of all that he wants to reveal.

Today was no different. As I rounded the corner of mile one, my vision strayed to a neighboring tree. Caught in the brambles of barren branches and contrasted against the brilliancy of the blue sky was a shimmering red bundle of something. The height of that something made its identification difficult, but as I drew closer, my suspicions were confirmed.

That bundle of "something" was, in fact, a bouquet of balloons. Valentine's balloons. Somebody's "something" had blown away in the night amidst the winds of a tempestuous storm. Somebody's expression of love left its intended home to now make its home amongst the tangled branches of a wintering tree. Somebody's surprise traversed the landscape to become my surprise, and I could not escape the sacred possibilities of such a revelation.

Love, in the form of a Valentine, made its way to this tree to teach me. Love tied itself to this tree to give me a blessing—a "Happy Valentine's Day" blessing. Love, battered by the winds of change, tangled itself in the middle of a tree whose grip was tight and who kept it there long enough for me to notice and to receive the benefits of such an engagement—better health, better mind, better spirit.

For the next two miles, my mind contemplated this modern-day parable that painted itself across my winter sky. The profundity of such a moment is not lost on me.

Two thousand years ago, love, in the form of a Son, made his way to a tree. Love tied himself to a tree to bring me a "Happy Valentine's Day" blessing. He scripted the message with the blood of his very own hands. Love, battered by the winds of the tempestuous storm, drove him to a purposeful tangling amidst thorns and brambles whose grip was tight and who kept him there long enough to finish love's completing work.

God's bouquet of love hung upon the winter tree, knowing that a spring's blossom awaited his full surrender. The air was crisp and cool, and yet the brilliancy of the Son reminded the world that death precedes the birth of a bloom. That beneath the branches boasting emptiness lie the buds that are readying themselves for a bursting forth that can only be described as miraculous.

A resurrection!

An Easter morning!

Better health. Better mind. Better spirit. Indeed, I would have missed it if had done what I wanted to do—I would have missed everything. I would have missed grace. I would have missed love. I would have missed Jesus.

I cannot consider such loss, for Jesus is all the world to me. I cannot go back and pretend that I do not know the truth, because long ago truth was revealed in my heart, and I have kept to his path ever since. I cannot forsake the understanding of Calvary's love, but there are days when I am prone to forget. Days when I need to break from the confines of my "want to," lace up my shoes, and push my flesh to a point of remembrance.

God is always faithful to reveal himself when I choose such an obedience. Today, he revealed himself through a bouquet of love that was tied to a tree. Tomorrow holds a revelation all its own. Until then, I will bask in the shadow of the blessing that hangs in surrender upon a neighboring branch. It is a blessing that says, "Happy Valentine's Day," this day and every day.

See him, hear him, and conceive the possibilities of such a gracious grace. What wondrous love is this! It is a love I want; thus, I pray—

Father, you are everything to me. You breathed your love over me as you tied your love to a tree at Calvary. No greater love have I ever known. It is a wondrous, undeserved, and lavish love that cannot be measured with words, music, or pictures. It can only be adequately known and expressed within

Peace on the road

the deep recesses of my being. You are there, God, for your Spirit lives within. Hear now my expression of love as it encompasses my frame and brings me to my knees in full surrender. You, alone, are worthy of such devotion. I receive your Valentine—your Son Jesus. I return my love to you. Where it is not perfect, perfect it, Lord. Better health, better mind, better spirit, that is what I want, so I pray for a heart to receive the fullness of such a gift. I stand ready to receive. Amen.

A further pause . . .

- Think of a time when God called you to an obedience exceeding your "want to." What were the results of your saying "yes" to his push?

- When in recent days has God sent you a special Valentine to remind you of his love? Describe.

- Take time to read John 12:20–36. How did Jesus respond to God's push for his "love" being tied to a tree? What benefits have we reaped because of his willing obedience to "do" his Father's will over his fleshly will?

Peace on the road

 a winter's run

Therefore, since we are surrounded by such a great cloud of witnesses, let us throw off everything that hinders and the sin that so easily entangles, and let us run with perseverance the race marked out for us.
—Hebrews 12:1

Do you run in the winter? In the cold and barren of a season that calls for cover and layers rather than exposure?

I run in the winter. I did so this morning. Not because I thrill to the feel of bone-chilling temperatures, but rather because I believe in its merits. The outward body may boast few results, but the inward—the heart, mind, and soul? Well, they believe in my obedience. They tell me that it's working on my behalf.

Even when it's cold. Even when I'm slow. Even when I cannot see the immediate benefits.

Running in frigid temperatures is a hard compliance. But running in the cold with a pace that warrants a snail's mentoring? Well, this adds a further difficulty for someone who desires a quick release from a long obedience.

I am a slow winter runner. Perhaps because of the bulky nature of my clothing. Perhaps because of the bulky nature of my soul.

There is a heaviness that comes with winter. Even though a tree's branches stand empty, their nakedness cries out for the blossoms of spring, the shading of summer, and the colors of fall. Why? Because when branches stand barren, the wind bites bitterly. The rain falls colder, and the snow blankets more heavily than when the branches are clothed with the foliage of warmer seasons.

That's the way of winter's embrace. It strips us and then requires us to wait for the redressing of spring. In the pause, we are left to manage the elements in hopes of an endurance that is strong enough and willing enough to carry us toward warmer days.

If we're not content to manage the cold through the refining warmth of God's fire—to allow winter the depth and purpose of her season and God's provision accordingly—then our load carries heavily. Thus, the bulky nature of a difficult obedience. Instead of permitting winter her stripping of us and, consequently, growing our trust for the eventual blossoms of spring, we have a propensity to blanket our nakedness with all manner of creature comforts. . . . Our plans. Our family. Our entertainment. Our vocations. Our responsibilities. Our worries. Our fears. Our hopes. Our prayers. Our problems. Our heartaches. Our joys. Our obedience. Our wills. Our _____.

Indeed, these are the makings of a bulky load regardless of the season. But when such cares are carried in winter, it is the load that slows our steps.

The problem?

Heavy doesn't companion well with runners who are pacing the cold of a long obedience. Winter was never designed to increase our load but rather to release it—to be the season of our sacred stripping. Winter doesn't intend for us to shoulder our heaviness. Instead, winter was designed to liberate us from our need to do so. To free us up to run the race with less burden. Less blankets. Less cover. Less worry.

This is the way of a winter's embrace. Unfortunately, many of us refuse its merits. Instead of acceptance, we regard our cold seasons as intrusive and unwarranted. Thus, the gloom and doom, as witnessed in the lives of countless people who cycle towards depression in winter rather than enjoying the brilliancy of God's seasons.

Every season possesses its worth. Whether the bud of spring, the heat of summer, the extravagant colors of fall, or the stripping of winter, seasons are designed by God with his specific purposes in mind, both in the literal and, especially, in the spiritual. To refuse them is to refuse their significance in our journeys towards a growing faith.

Right now, I'm running in winter, and I want to run it better—with less of my burden and more of God's strength. To do so, I must surrender my limbs to their stripping and my heart to God's refining.

Perhaps you, too, are experiencing the heaviness of a winter season. The days are short, and the nights seem ever so long. Your load grows heavier with every dip of the thermometer.

God's understands your burden. What he asks of you and me is that he be allowed to empty our branches so that we might effectively run the race that he has marked out for us—in front of us and all because of us, until we cross the finish line of our forever and the cold of our winter springs into the bloom of our resurrection.

Soon, and very soon, we will have run the cycle of our seasons to their fruition. It seems a long time in coming, but it is only a moment from now—a breath or two between what currently "is" and what is soon to be. God holds the calendar from beginning to end.

May his willing strength be our portion to finish our seasons well, to run them lighter, and to welcome them as he intended. Thus, I pray—

Peace on the road

Keep me running, Father, in all seasons, with a faith that focuses towards the finish rather than staying mired in the temporal. When winter blows her bitter winds, when my heart and soul know the barrenness and chill of a difficult stripping, give me the courage to withstand the process, to see its merits, and to embrace its purpose. Release me from my heavy burdens so that I will be able to run with the swift assurance of what awaits me at the end of the journey. You are the embrace at the end of my seasons. Shadow my pace with your sustaining power and grace until I get there. Amen.

A further pause . . .

- How would you describe your current season of running? The cold and barren of winter, the blossom of spring, the hot of summer, or the colorful release of fall?

- Give some descriptive words about winter, such as cold, dark, lonely, etc.

- What parallels can you see between your description of a winter season and a winter season of the soul?

- Ecclesiastes 3:1–8 paints a vivid portrait about the purpose behind our many seasons. Please read it and record any ways you find "winter" within King Solomon's painting.

- Why do you think we are given our seasons of winter? Can you see the tracing of God's hand and purpose therein?

Peace on the road

a gracious plenty

Our desire is not that others might be relieved while you are hard pressed, but that there might be equality. At the present time your plenty will supply what they need, so that in turn their plenty will supply what you need. Then there will be equality, as it is written: "He who gathered much did not have too much, and he who gathered little did not have too little."

—2 Corinthians 8:13–15

I saw it this morning. Right in the place where I've been seeing it all summer long. A bag filled with a garden's growings. A gracious plenty offered to me and my family by a retired couple who understand God's principle of surplus as outlined in Paul's letter to the Corinthians.

I don't know this couple well. They only recently moved here; but in the time since their arrival, we've managed a few chats amidst my morning runs and have discovered a mutual love for God and for garden produce. They've instructed me that the hanging bags on the mailbox are meant for my retrieval. Gladly I receive them, and today was no exception.

It has me thinking, pondering about a heart that gives from the overflow of a garden. A luscious plenty that's been soiled and seeded, tilled and tended with a harvest in mind. Rather than hoard and shelve their produce, my new friends have decided to share the wealth of their garden's growings.

I like that. I like the surprise of seeing my bag hanging on their mailbox and knowing I've been thought about with the picking. This is the way of an abundant heart.

An abundant heart grows a surplus and then, out of that overflow, shares the extra with others in need. And while there are, perhaps, more pressing needs in my own life than that of garden produce, I am tendered and touched by the hearts of a people who understand that giving always yields a return—if not in the immediate, then somewhere down the road.

As I examine my own life, I look for the plenty, for the extra measure of a garden's growth that could be shared with others.

What about you? Where does your plenty lie this day? Look at your hands, your heart, your giftings, and your wallet. Examine them under the light of Calvary's grace and tell me, where is your plenty?

Plenty. The word "perisseuma" in the Greek, meaning, "to abound; surplus; abundance in which one delights; that which fills the heart; that which is leftover; remains; residue."[13]

We all have an existing plenty. Regardless of our outpouring—whether financially, physically, spiritually, emotionally—there exists a surplus somewhere within. A plenty that is meant to be shared for the benefit and the building up of the body of Christ. We don't often feel this to be the case, for we are a busy and tired people with an output level that leaves us saddled with our weariness.

So often we crawl into our beds and pray for the strength to walk another day, giving little attention to any needs other than the ones that frame our flesh. Left unattended and unnoticed, our needs become our blinding, and our plenty is shelved and buried beneath the weight of an inward focus.

This is the way of a selfish heart—a perfected "taking" that harbors the lie that we have nothing left in our reserves to offer. No surplus or residue therein for the sharing. No bags to hang on the mailbox. No garden's growth and, therefore, no produce to share with our neighbors.

Today, I host a selfish heart, and it's not healthy. And while God allows me my weariness with a depth of understanding and healing that only he can offer, he expects me to keep an outward focus, even during my times of refueling.

My resources may be limited on all fronts, but there is still a surplus in reserve. His name is Jesus, and he is my overflow. The residue of his abiding presence can be seen, felt, and tasted through this heart of mine. My plenty may be different from yours, but its seeding comes through the same grace. He far outweighs the temporal offering of our hands.

We can give our neighbors Jesus, even when we feel that we have little to offer. We do so through our words, our simple acts of kindness, our attitudes, our compassion, our prayers, and our hanging out of all manner of a sacred garden's produce that is meant for the taking and for the closer examination of God's eternal abundance.

You may feel that your garden's harvest is lean and sparse, but there is always a bag of God's plenty ready for the hanging. Yours is uniquely created with your gifts in mind. Your plenty will fill the need of another through the overflow of a Father's love. Mine will do the same. Together we can feed the world with the produce of our gracious God.

Accordingly, keep to it. Keep tending to your garden and keep packaging up God's blessings to pass on to those who are dropping by for a taste. I know it's not always easy. Even today, I painfully struggle with my own offering. But God's love compels me to do so. Perhaps somewhere in the doing, my meager surplus will be enough to equal your hungering need. Like my neighbors, I hang Jesus out for the entire world to see. And he, my friends, is the gracious plenty who is more than enough to assuage a world's hunger with the finest bread of heaven.

Let it be so for each one of us today. May the eternal seeding of the Eternal One produce a harvest rich and plentiful in and through your heart. From my mailbox to yours, thank you for taking the time to pause at mine. You have been purposefully thought about with this "picking." Thus, I pray—

In the name of the Father who seeds us with his love, and of the Son who nourishes us with the truth, and of the abiding and breathing Holy Spirit who grows us as we go, Amen and Amen.

Peace on the road

A further pause . . .

    How is your garden growing this week? What offering from your heart is hanging on your mailbox today?

    Read the following scriptures and record how a "gracious plenty" was provided for God's people:

    Leviticus 23:15–22

    Ruth 2:5–18

    Nehemiah 8:9–12

    Matthew 14:15–21

    List some practical ways you can offer Jesus to others this week.

a morning's glory

> *Our fathers disciplined us for a little while as they thought best; but God disciplines us for our good, that we may share in his holiness.*
>
> —Hebrews 12:10

This morning, I almost didn't do what I needed to do.

Almost.

But I didn't. Instead, I did what I needed to do, and in doing so, I got a taste of some morning glory!

I jogged four miles, and I am the better because of it.

I made the choice to partake in a discipline that's been following me for over twenty years. Most days, I hate the doing. It is a painful dig within the soil of my stubborn will. Discipline is like that. It rarely feels good at the time, but in the end, it usually works toward my good. And while my outward doesn't necessarily mirror the fruits of my hard laboring, my inward boasts the beauty of my commitment . . .

Heart health.

As it is with the temporal, so it is with my eternal.

I've got a heart that needs strengthening and a faith that needs walking. It's what I need to do, and on most days, it's what I want to do. But there are those occasions when my faith walk seems better left untouched—unchallenged and untamed by life's "daily," because, quite frankly, life's "daily" wears heavily upon my stubborn will.

No matter. Long ago, I made the decision to reposition my will behind God's. In doing so, I signed up for a life that chooses best interest over preferred interest. And as much as I am prone to the latter, it is the former that keeps me on the road towards heart health.

When the health of the heart takes precedence over the emotions of the heart, God is faithful to honor such obedience with a measure of maturing that cannot be attained otherwise. We may not see it, feel it, touch it, or taste it in the immediate, but down the road, it will be our strengthened portion when we most need the power of its witness.

A walking faith is a difficult faith. It means that we surrender our ideas about how we think it ought to breathe and, instead, receive the deep breath of the Holy Spirit, who companions our steps, no matter how sharp and hard the path. It means drinking him in, even when our preferences lead our lust towards the ladle of another well. It means keeping to the Word and believing in its effectual and accomplishing power, even when the script reads seemingly void of purpose.

It means getting up, day in and evening out, and living the truth of who we are as children of the Most High God, even when our preferred inclination leans toward the snooze button.

Fully living our sacred adoption as God's children is our good and gracious requirement if we are ever to share in his holiness and reach our perfected end. This is the overriding truth that keeps me on the path, not my emotions or my feelings. They've run the show for most of my life and almost always run counterproductive to God's agenda for me.

Thus, I am learning to deny them their unhealthy portion of influence. Instead, I am filling my life with the discipline of Jesus—as Nietzsche and, later, Eugene Peterson wrote, "a long obedience in the same direction."[14] It doesn't sound too exciting, does it? In fact, to most it sounds rather boring and walks even more laborious. But there again, it matters not how it sounds or feels. What matters is the choice to embrace the journey.

I am finding that with such a decision comes some of the most fantastic growth I have ever known as a Christian. Why? Because choices that seed on behalf of the heart always yield long-term benefits—a lasting harvest of peace and righteousness that will carry this soul to its perfected end.

This is what I'm after. This is why I will keep to the road and to the run, even when my preference leans toward the snooze button. Jesus Christ is the great finisher and completer of my faith journey; thus, I will keep repositioning my will behind his until he brings me home to my forever.

I don't know how this strikes you today. Many of you are weary. Many of you are in the middle of making some hard decisions, perhaps even living the effects of some bad ones. Some of you stand at the edge of a road, wondering if the walk ahead is worth the process. Some of you stand at the end of a road, looking back with regrets and wishing for a do-over. A blessed few are skipping along with the pure contentment of trusting in Jesus for the unseen. And a gracious many, unfortunately, are hitting the snooze button one more time in hopes of waking up to a better day.

No matter. What does matter, however, is what you choose to do with your now. What will be the next step in your journey towards heart health? Our steps matter, and together, we can do this thing. We can walk home to Jesus with a measure of sure victory, because we are his chosen dwelling. Rarely will it breathe easily, but always it will breathe with the hope of heaven.

Peace for the Journey

Therefore, strengthen your feeble arms and weak knees. Make level paths for your feet, so that the lame may not be disabled, but rather healed. Make every effort to live in peace with all men and to be holy; without holiness no one will see the Lord. See to it that no one misses the grace of God.

—Hebrews 12:12–15

Indeed, let us not miss the grace of God or the magnificent glory of a morning run! See to it, friends. Thus, I pray—

Keep us to the path of our long obedience, Lord, which leads in only one direction—home to you. Strengthen our frames to do that which our souls need to do, rather than what our emotions cry out to do. Show us the beauty and lavish expression of your heart so that we in turn will choose to tend to ours. And when all seems too hard and too costly, fill our frames with the wind of your Spirit, who breathes sacred perspective over all our "seeming" until it fades beneath the truth of our becoming. Thank you, Father, for your good discipline that is leading me on to my completion. And while it sometimes hurts and requires a hard humbling, I know that you intend it for my holiness. Thus, I gladly yield to your staff and to your rod this day. Amen.

Peace on the road

A further pause . . .

- List some of the fleshly disciplines that are a part of your daily routine. What is the purpose behind those disciplines?

- What are some of the spiritual disciplines that are a part of your daily routine? What is the purpose behind them?

- Consider your "efforts" at both. Which is easier? Describe.

- Take time to read the account of Daniel's daily obedience as found in Daniel 6. Describe his obedience in verse 10. What was the outcome of Daniel's difficult obedience in verses 22, 26–28?

Conclusion: a leaving peace

Peace I leave with you; my peace I give you. I do not give to you as the world gives. Do not let your hearts be troubled and do not be afraid.

—John 14:27

I found some peace this morning. He found me, too. I'm not sure how that works—how much of the finding is mine and how much of it belongs to God. But when our mutual pursuits collide, when the fragments of my frailty intersect with the entirety of his holiness, peace breathes. Peace rules. Peace companions, because peace is God's intention.

Jesus' peace is a leaving peace.

He didn't take it with him two thousand years ago when he departed from this earthen sod to return to his Father's throne in heaven. He left peace as our portion; he did not leave it in part, but in fullness through the power of his Holy Spirit.

When Jesus told his followers about his soon and coming departure, undoubtedly their hearts were burdened by grief and confusion. It is the same for us. Anytime we perceive our Jesus to be absent from our "routine and normal" we, too, are prone to our uncertainty until we can no longer find the thread of peace that links us back to our faith. Unless our peace is anchored within the truth of Jesus' offering of peace, our lingering chaos lasts long and hard and keeps us from experiencing the immediate intention of a Father's gift.

The disciples were at a distinct disadvantage compared to us, although we often think of them as more blessed for having walked and talked with Jesus and for being the front row witnesses to his miraculous. No, in that moment of hearing Jesus' forecast concerning his future, their troubled hearts didn't have the benefit of the one thing we now possess . . .

Hindsight—a backward glance into sacred history as we now know it.

Peace for the Journey

We see Jesus' cycle of life and understand the reason for his cross. We are the benefactors of such an understanding. But when Christ spoke to the disciples concerning his death and his resurrection, their momentary pain kept them shackled to the confusion of the cross instead of pushing them ahead to see the promise of their forever.

It was a moment worthy of the spoken word and the spoken Presence of that word.

Peace . . .

Not as the world gives, but as the Father gives. And that giving, friends, exceeds this world's idea of a marketable peace. God's peace profits better: More than the eye can see. More than the ear can hear. More than the mind can conceive. And sometimes, more than our faith can believe.

God's immeasurably more will always trump the seen and the measurable. The gifts from our Father's hands are the seeding of our tomorrows. He gives with the future in mind. His gifts boast an eternal reach, because eternity is his to give, and peace is ours to live.

We need not look any further for the seemingly unattainable. If Jesus is our Savior, then we contain within us the absolute attainable. Peace is our constant and abiding companion for the road beneath our feet. He leads us home to our forever, where our faith will finally give way to sight, and we will behold the fullness of God's peace face-to-face, for always.

Who can fathom the glorious riches of our then—of our now? May the leaving peace of God be the holy intersection of our hearts for the journey, this day and forever. Thus, a final prayer—

> *Jesus, you are our peace. Keep us to the road of peace. Harbor our thoughts in the depth of your constant and abiding peace who lives within. When we are tempted to search elsewhere—to pull out the wallet and to purchase peace at the going rate—drop us to our knees in thankfulness for the price that has already been paid for your gift of lasting peace. Walk through the door of our hearts, Lord, and speak your words of peace over our journeys. Give according to your "immeasurably more" and not according to our requests for less. You, Father, have made us for more; thus, we bow to receive our portion from your hand this day. Amen.*

Endnotes

1. Robert Morgan, *Then Sings My Soul* (Nashville: Thomas Nelson, 2003), 78–79.
2. Baker & Carpenter, *The Complete Word Study Dictionary Old Testament* (Chattanooga, TN: AMG Publishers, 2003), 245.
3. Ibid., 956.
4. Ibid.
5. *Zondervan NIV Study Bible* (Grand Rapids, MI: Zondervan, 2002), 30.
6. Spiros Zodhiates, *The Complete Word Study Dictionary New Testament* (Chattanooga, TN: AMG Publishing, 1992), 1205.
7. Ibid., 1039.
8. Ibid., 996.
9. Baker & Carpenter, *The Complete Word Study Dictionary Old Testament* (Chattanooga, TN: AMG Publishers, 2003), 245.
10. Spiros Zodhiates, *The Complete Word Study Dictionary New Testament* (Chattanooga, TN: AMG Publishers, 1992), 1210–1211.
11. Ibid., 1187–1188.
12. Ibid., 1106.
13. Ibid., 1150.
14. Eugene Peterson, *A Long Obedience in the Same Direction* (Downers Grove, IL: Intervarsity Press, 2000), 17.

NyreePress

NyreePress Literary Group
"Publishing Life for Families"
www.nyreepress.com
www.buglovebooks.com
Twitter: @nyreepress

www.ingramcontent.com/pod-product-compliance
Lightning Source LLC
Chambersburg PA
CBHW080345300426
44110CB00019B/2513